the

PHANTOMS

of

SURREALISM

Neil Coombs

with essays by
Krzysztof Fijalkowski
Catriona McAra

Published by
Dark Windows Press
72 Llandudno Road
Rhos-on-Sea
LL28 4EJ
UK

www.darkwindows.co.uk
info@darkwindows.co.uk

First Edition 2012

0123456789

Printed in the UK

ISBN-13: 978-0-9571644-4-4

Design and layout by Neil Coombs

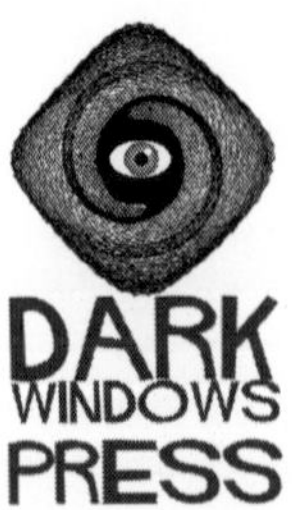

Contents

Introduction

The photomontage pieces that form the core of *The Phantoms of Surrealism* project are built around a repeating grid of 15 rectangles into which photographs from a specific location are inserted to form a spirit or 'phantom' of place. Each *Phantom* is from a different location and each site chosen either relates to the history of surrealism in Britain and Europe or has personal resonances for the artist. The works are both an interpretation of landscape and locus as well as an opportunity to explore the history of the surrealist movement in Britain; how the surrealist landscape is explored, not for its picturesque or romantic aspects but for its psychological and visionary resonance.

In order to create the work for this project, Neil Coombs travelled to a range of locations in the UK during 2011 - 2012 where he collected a body of photographs that have been used in the construction of the *Phantom* photmontages. The *Phantom* works have been produced as large scale digital prints for exhibition but they also have a life as small scale *Phantom Trading Cards*. These micro and macro artworks have been exhibited and distributed in a range of locations and formats and their "seething potential" is discussed in Krzysztof Fijalkowski's essay *The Ghosts of Neil Coombs*.

This book also explores some of Coombs's other works: In her essay *Story Without a Name - for Neil Coombs*, Catriona McAra examines his collage series *A Pictorial History of the British Isles* (2010). These works (along with the series *A Brief History of Art and Desire*) utilise collage to engage with landscape and art history. The final examples of Coombs's work in this book reflect on a certain kind of obsessive photographic practice (*Photography: Disease of the Eye*) and it can be seen that the *Phantom* works have emerged from the marriage of these two concerns.

As the *Phantoms* continue their relentless, compulsive progress they will develop a life of their own. You, dear reader, are invited to create and liberate your own photomontages using the template provided.

We look forward to meeting your *Phantoms*...

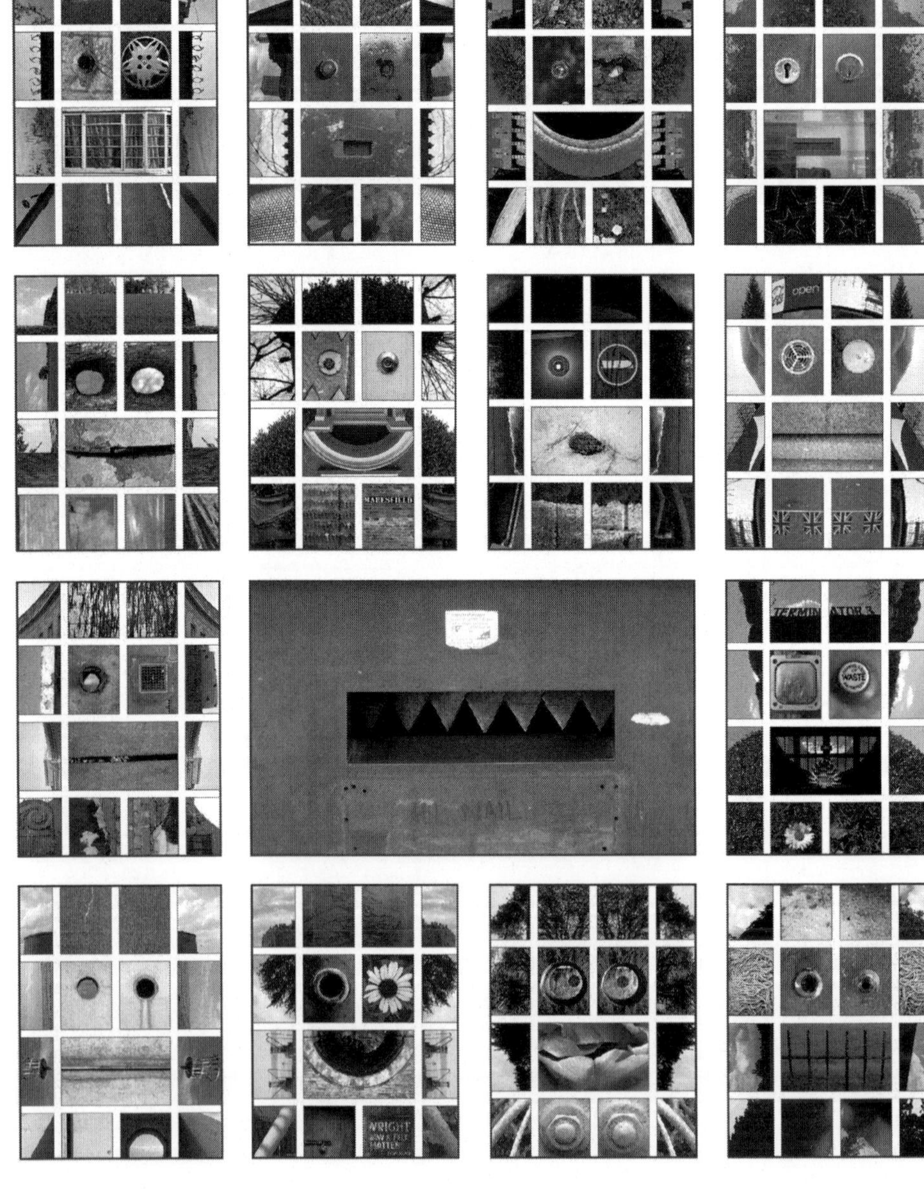

The Ghosts of Neil Coombs

Krzysztof Fijalkowski

Questions rather than statements, Neil Coombs's series of *Phantoms* reveals a hidden order of beings that might rear up at us from every street corner or urban construction. From the incident we might have no more than glanced at and passed over come the pieces, half figment, half fragment, of an anatomical jigsaw waiting to slot together and form the hieratic creatures that dwell within each location Coombs visits on his restless journeys.

In tension between the adoption of a rigorous, standardized format in which each discovered and photographed element is locked into the game of fifteen rectangles – fourteen portrait, one landscape – but where this identical grid is the very way to find that no two apparitions are the same, the Phantoms are a conscious continuation of nearly century-old practices in collage and photomontage, the twentieth (and still it would seem the early twenty-first) century's defining visual representation. We live, the Berlin Dadaists revealed just at the end of the First World War (Picasso and Braque had known this already a few years earlier) in a collage environment. The city is an assemblage of juxtaposed fragments, multiple, discontinuous; glimpses caught in a mirror ball and temporarily hung together by our organizing gaze at each moment, ready to be supplanted by the next. Newspapers, magazines (both then only recently starting to be illustrated with photographs), films with their edited montage; streets as a jumble of forms, functions and signs; the jostle of sensory information as you walk the pavement; the overheard conversation at your side phasing with street sounds, placards and shop windows clamouring attention, the panoply of decisions (café, cinema, shop, street), the buzzing ideologies of commodities.

Dada *photomonteurs* fed off the noise of situations and environments – of media environments as much as the concrete world, so much was the everyday beginning to be made of both at once – lapping up experience and revelling in the heteroclite: difference and disarray is the very stuff of the collages of Hannah Höch, Raoul Hausmann or

(early) John Heartfield (Höch's work over the following decades is
particularly apposite here, with her playful and disturbing reconstructions of face, body and identity through the deft overlay of fashion
plates and commodity advertising). Yet this chaos is also caught at a
moment when everything, for a second, might also make sense, when
the giddy animation of signs and images momentarily and apparently
by chance (ha! chance…) joins up to make something recognisable,
like a miraculous alignment of planets on the scale of a sheet of paper.
Photography, eighty years old but now saturating and defining the urban condition since that new reproduction technologies had made its
proliferation in the mass media ubiquitous, enabled the Dada *monteur*
to plunge into a world of images that was both dizzying in its variety
and which revealed through their appropriations and reassignments
in collage the absurd or cynical codes and ideologies that lay beneath
the spectacle of stuff. Dada photomontage is recognisable today as the
beginnings of a viral colonisation of the media environment.

If Berlin Dada photomontage proposes an absurd and sarcastic ency-
clopaedia of montaged situations, surrealism's theories of the image,
explored in its poems, paintings, photographs and collages, began to
read these juxtapositions not so much as temporary and derisory ironic accidents, but as keys to a deeper understanding of the mechanisms
of the mind and the subterranean knowledge kept secret by places and
things. Chance encounters, particularly in the city – unexpected finds
in flea markets and junk shops, the sign on a backstreet business, a
familiar stranger glimpsed on the opposite pavement – are no longer
random events but meaningful signals, beckoning the participant to
decode them as one might puzzle over a dream. For surrealism, the
apparently bizarre incongruities of these coincidences and collisions
are the very guarantee that something is happening, that some emer-
gent but yet to be understood meaning tugs insistently at the sleeve,
at the corner of our vision, apparently beyond our control in the
outside world yet joined by a filament to our imagination, memory
and destiny. That delicious shiver we feel is the electricity of external
necessity, as André Breton suggests in *Mad Love*, making its way
through the human unconscious. Breton's first *Surrealist Manifesto*
of 1924, still for the moment worrying over the written word rather

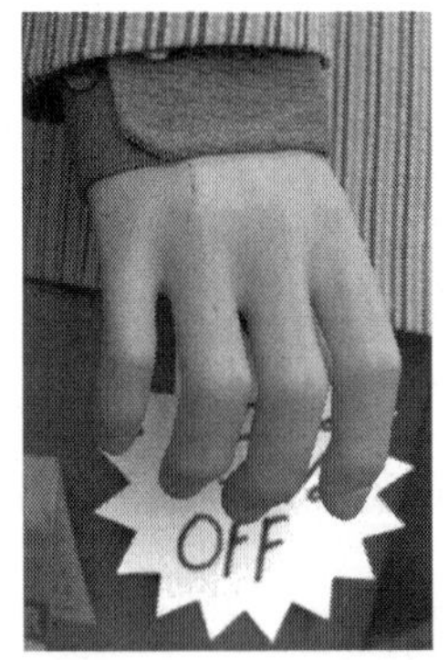

than the visual realm, places its bets on this energy of difference, on the electrical potential of things aligned that cannot be together yet mustn't be kept apart (that familiar but irresistible tale of star-crossed lovers). Quoting Pierre Reverdy, Breton writes:

> The image is a pure creation of the mind.
> It cannot be born from a comparison but from a juxtaposition of two more or less distant realities.
> The more the relationship between the two juxtaposed realities is distant and true, the stronger the image will be...

And later, in his own words this time,

> The value of the image depends on the beauty of the spark obtained; it is, consequently, a function of the difference of potential between the two conductors.

Generators of such images, insisting they have been found rather than made, surrealist poetry or collage are at one level nothing but machines for making these thrilling sparks, like those little hand-held metal toys you can still buy (I remember adoring them as a child) where you push a plunger to whir a gritted wheel from which tiny flashes of fire leap behind coloured cellophane; useless, perfect.

Breton, following Reverdy, names the image's components as 'distant realities', since their jarring encounter emphasises their apparent incompatibility; yet they seem not so distant in another sense, since they have been found in the same location, or have crashed into each other in a single spot; they are gathered together by place, by a different order of belonging: a belonging of space and affinity not category, of a connection derived from material experience not reasoned deduction. This sense of collage's collision in a particular location ('the plane of non-agreement') is underlined by Max Ernst's definition of the medium in Beyond Painting:

> The complete transmutation, followed by a pure act, as that of love, will make itself known every time the conditions are

rendered favourable by the given facts: the coupling of two realities, irreconcilable in appearance, upon a plane which apparently does not suit them.

Something about place, then, saturates these encounters, makes the access to the irrational and the unconscious sought by surrealism's appeal to the image seem to happen through the particular doorway or passage of one privileged spot, just as the Phantoms are insistently tied to their locations and seem so often to feature images of apertures, ingress and thresholds, their grids suggesting the grills of a Georgian or Victorian glass-panelled front door or window.

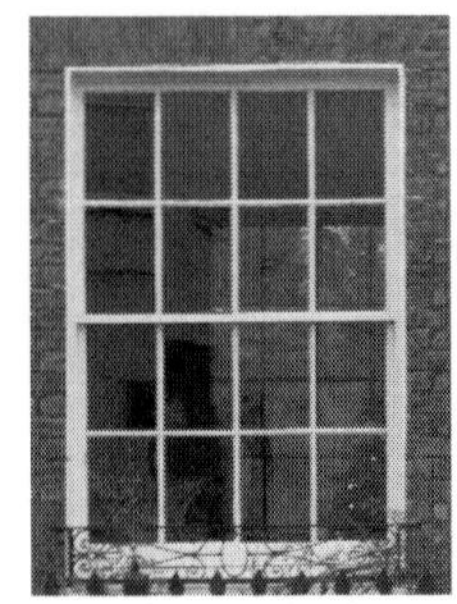

Dada collage, the surrealist image of the 1920s: these are ideas that relate to a world whose whispers we catch but whose times are long gone. How might this be configured for the early twenty-first century? Does, it matter, for example, that the Phantoms are made out of digital images, downloaded and manipulated within the parameters of screen and software rather than developed in a darkroom and cut and pasted in paper or card? I tend to be more convinced by accounts that see digital technologies as a change in the pace and distribution of mid twentieth-century image technologies rather than a fundamental shift in vision and production. But the digital image's possibilities for drastic shifts in scale – zooming in the fragment, juxtaposing the tiny and the immense until neither provide any reference – seem to be particularly foregrounded in the Phantoms, where an entire tree sprouts its hair next to a rivet for an eye, a whole skyline sits on top of an architectural detail, and the camera's zoom and macro functions work overtime (just as the material form of Phantoms can't seem to settle down, ranging all the way from hand-sized cards to giant poster-scale prints). What has shifted most, perhaps, and in ways that are hardest to gauge, is something one might term the economy of collage. Once upon a time making collages meant generating the raw material of hundreds of clippings and snippets, piles of possible elements cut from the print sources and then tried out in myriad configurations before one particular arrangement imposed itself – sometimes not the one you had expected, and indeed often the things done accidentally were the most surprising and effective – and you took the chance with the glue, leaving a pile of unused elements as a kind of reservoir of potential next works. Now, making collages from digital sources means never having to quite decide definitively which things to use; digital 'cutting' or 'pasting' (the terms survive at least) are no longer a risk, since each step, each source image, can always be retrieved, and rather than piles of scraps, what's generated is different versions, multiple incarnations, from which the definitive (but perhaps never 'finished') work can be selected.

A sense of the Phantoms' inter-changeability and provisional nature, each one seething with different potential elements and arrangements stacked behind its form, seems built into their logic; every Phantom owes its tension partly to the sense of its possible others, of the absolute but temporary nature of each ghost of a place. This is in part, I suspect, the result of the rigorous and standardised grid format the Phantoms adopt, keying them to something old and something resolutely contemporary at the same time. In Dada and surrealist collage grids are relatively rare: for the former, for example, there are Jean Arp's *Squares Arranged According to the Laws of Chance*, though these works approach a pure if organic geometry, usually leaving out any image; or the chessboards of Duchamp and Man Ray. For surrealism, there are Victor Brauner's satirical body morphologies of 1933-34, some of Magritte's word-image lessons from the late 1920s onwards, Dali's photomontage *The Phenomenon of Ecstasy* (1933), the stacks of surrealists' faces around a picture of Germaine Berton or Magritte's *La Femme cachée* of 1929 in the pages of surrealist journals, or Man Ray's *Surrealist Chessboard* of 1934 in which once again photographs of surrealist group members are arranged in a tight box structure. But all of these use the grid for comparison, juxtaposition or array, rather than construct a single image from fragments, and the only close comparison to the Phantoms are Gherasim Luca's 'cubomanias' invented during the war in Bucharest, and in which source images would be guillotined into regular squares, jumbled up and re-assembled into troubling tessellations of fragmented representation, seething with violence and erotic tensions. Rosalind Krauss, in her seminal essay of 1979 on the grid (and from which Dada and surrealist grids are notably absent), sees it as embodying modern art's claims for disrupting

narrative, bringing together the material and the universal, and above
all elevating ideas to the level of myth, that structure designed pre-
cisely to suspend opposing things together. So far so promising, but
while the notion of the grid as organizational play, as schizophrenic
window, might hold some sway for the *Phantoms* or the cubomania
and the repetitive or serial nature of their practice, they have no interest in the kind of formal games the grid represents for modernist art,
but seek instead an order that is really a screen for another category of
knowledge, the open structure of an archive rather than the discipline
of a parade ground. Play (as theorised for example by Johan Huizinga
in his *Homo Ludens* of 1938), with its paradoxical generative principle
of the promise of freedom within structure, of a fresh logic that breaks
with all existing logic, that tests and perfects change, seems closer to
the rationale of the Phantoms, whose organisation is rigorous only the
better to be forever multiple and unstable. Coombs' idea of reconfig-
uring the *Phantoms* as trading cards, bringing their icons back to the
intuitive economies and inventive play of children, only confirms this
tendency.

Behind these apparitions stands another shadow, that of the sixteenth
century mannerist painter Arcimboldo, and then crowding behind
come other, seventeenth century and later, masters of the bizarre and
fantastic double-image arrangements of nature and the figure, of
the thing that is something else as well – Joos de Momper, Bracelli,
Grandville. Like archaic precursors of collage and rarer than one
might imagine, their works burrow into our unconscious and popu-
late it with living landscapes that threaten to get up and walk; with
pots and pans, piles of food or journeymen's wares drawn together
into humanoid form; with nature and the planets dressed in the finery
of the aristocracy, or reversals in hierarchies of established relationships (fish angling for men, flower sprites). In Arcimboldo every
object, every casual arrangement of possessions seems liable suddenly
to animate itself into some being or pagan deity, a springing up of the
world of things most brilliantly brought to life in Jan Švankmajer's
animation *Dimensions of Dialogue* (1982), where each category of
knowledge represented by its constituent tools and commodities has
its wicked revenge on its rivals, until all that's left is a pulpy human

clay: we are what we use. In the Phantoms, the systems of knowledge seem more benign, less prone to turning on their fellows, ready to swap body parts rather than joust for them; a calmness and expectancy familiar from de Momper and Arcimboldo, and in the face of each extraordinary resemblance is a kind of childish elation mixed with antediluvian certainty: 'see, you knew all along I was here'.

Against the grain of our usual frames of order – what kinds of things belong with what kinds of other things – just as Arcimboldo's vision is at one level all about classification and the limits of knowledge, here a secret set of assignations and relationships asserts itself, and objects, places and details find a deeper form, neighbourhood and meaning. The figure, the face become the measure of all things, whether in acknowledgement that all categories, all notions derive in the end from our own projections ('nature' exists as a concept only because we call it so), or because behind every place, every building, every texture there really lies some dormant spirit. A delicately-balanced symmetry, emphasised by the Phantoms' grid and, like all good symmetries, always slightly out of true, always not quite, rules and defines while never properly deciding: left side or right side, distaff or spear, who knows how the binaries of these creatures fall? Something about the comforting yet profoundly strange idea of vertical symmetry is tapped into, creating upright, sentient beings from the humblest materials, and that primeval Rorschach arrangement of shapes signalling presence (a tiny baby will smile at two eyes and a mouth scribbled crudely on a piece of paper).

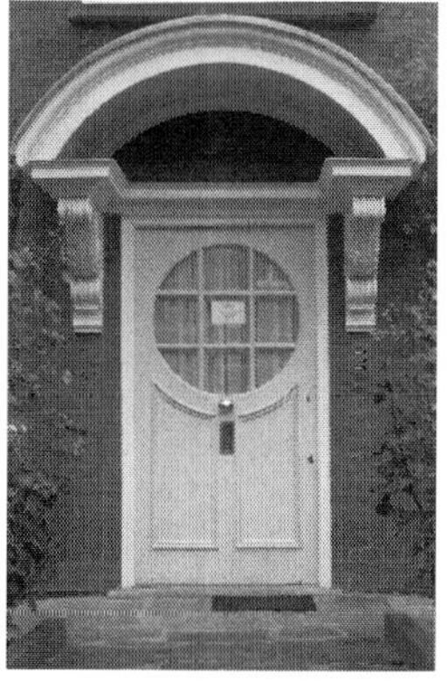

Here is the realm of the uncanny: the familiar, the all-too-familiar, revealed in a deft moment as the very opposite of expectations, producing the thrill and anxiety of being faced with our own unconscious fears and drives discovered in the outside world. Freud includes phenomena such as doubling and the uncertainty over whether forms such as mannequins are human or artificial among his categorization of the *unheimlich* (the German rendition of the uncanny: the 'unhomely'), to which we might add for the Phantoms the uncanniness of entire buildings apparently possessed of spirit and intelligence, familiar from haunted house storylines in films (we note that Freud's

own house in Maresfield Gardens earns a Phantom of its own). The
uncanny, like many of the most revealing modes of explaining the
world, owes its power in part to its ambivalence, to its ability to elicit
opposing responses: fear and fascination, elation and dread. And are
these Phantoms a product of growth or entropy (just as *Dimensions of
Dialogue* troubles us with its tension between collapse and construction), are they the portent of an army massing under our noses or the
last remnants of a decaying race? Perhaps, like the totems or deities of
many cultures, they are neither inherently benign nor aggressive, not
forming or disappearing but just there, eternally and without malice
or proclivity, beyond the horizon of our own sorry binaries.

One of the oppositions we cannot help ascribing the Phantoms,
nevertheless, is the delicate symmetry between the natural and the
social that informs the fibre of their being, even if it is a natural tamed
by the social (trees from parks and gardens, bits of sky framed by
rooftops) and a social marked by the weathering and organic growth
of nature (natural materials turned to human use, worn surfaces,
seething marks and furrows on the built environment). Here object
and subject grow confused, the balance between what was already
there and what has been deliberately created flicks back and forth,
and a kind of giddy vitalism invades every surface, building and plant.
Desire, anxiety, both projected onto and received from the everyday
material world, disturbing the convenient difference we'd like to
maintain between our environments and our selves; 'soul' (for want of
a better word, though there's no transcendence here) leaks everywhere.
On the one hand a kind of naïve anthropomorphism rules the Phantoms, willing every object and structure into a life of its own (a world-
view familiar to all of us from the dawn of our entry into language
thanks to those delightful children's books and fairy tales where trees
speak and cutlery gets married). But by the same token, the body, our
self, becomes a place, inhabitable, exotic, a landscape of territories
and human geology. Embodiments of the notion of genius loci, the
'spirit of place', the Phantoms draw together all of the memories and
emotions of location as alive to our passage through it, in the face of
our contemporary perception that our places, our cities, are becoming
either more and more the same, or are turning into theme-park simu-

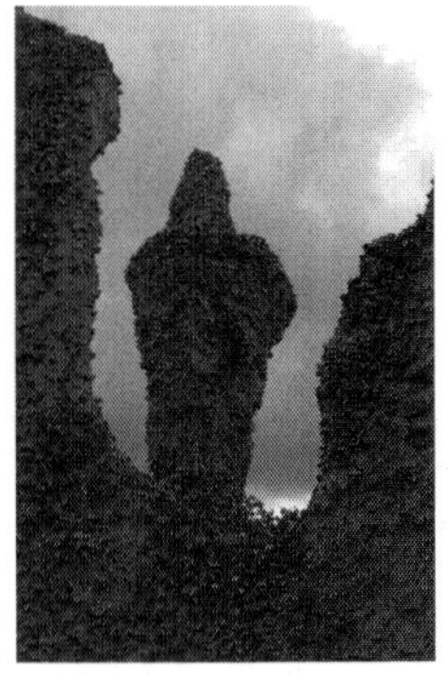

lacra of a once genuine experience. Their unnerving lesson is in part that we, too, are made of bits, are a temporary yet profound arrangement of heteroclite objects, fragments and memories coming together for a moment, invisible to all but those canny enough to acknowledge our being. If Phantoms of location and (urban) landscape exist only because we project our identity and desire onto them, is it possible that we too, in return, are nothing but reversed projections of that landscape's identity, figments dreamed by place? The Phantoms give material weight to the idea that identity saturates place, doubles it so exactly as to make it invisible under normal light; that the unconscious lives somewhere in particular, it dwells, rather than just orbiting the mind. Outside, inside; body, city: the collapse and coalescence of these categories is profoundly troubling, since it would force us to rethink our entire relationship to the world; the Phantoms, like some Easter Island statues for the so-called modern world, mute, terrible remnants heralding a message even they have forgotten how to utter, stand as sentinels for the disintegration of our world view.

Restless, mobile, even as their massive form makes the thought of them moving one of their most unsettling aspects, the Phantoms are themselves the product of wanderings and dispersals. Both the evidence and, at one level, the purpose of Coombs' journeys around Britain and beyond to seek out for himself the significant places of alternate histories – most particularly the history of surrealism and its resonances – they mark a passage, figure reconstructions of location and memory. Underneaths, reversals, inversions, they are the products and the evidence of a kind of haunting, where Coombs himself has become both the ghost and a kind of photographer-medium, summoning the spirits of place. A ghostliness stalks his project.

**Farley Farm
Sussex**

The home of Roland Penrose and Lee Miller
that became one of the key meeting places
in Britain for some of the leading figures
in the world of Modern Art. Pablo Picasso,
Max Ernst, Joan Miro, Man Ray, Echaurren
Matta and Antoni Tapies visited Farley Farm
and their spirits persist here alongside those
of the British artists Eileen Agar, Kenneth
Armitage, William Turnbull, John Craxton
and Richard Hamilton.

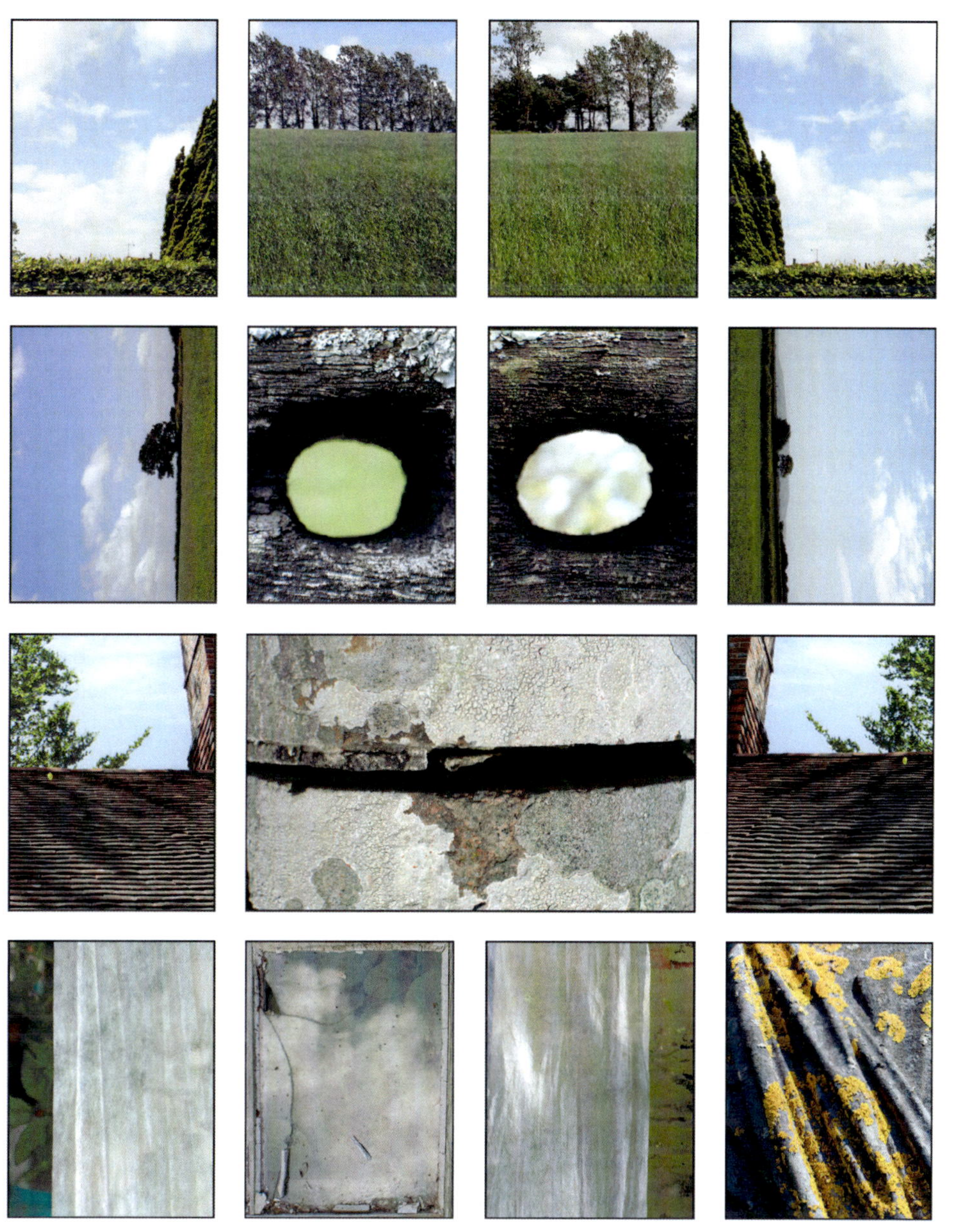

The Phantom of Farley Farm (2012)
digital print on aluminum 104 x 84 cm

Shepperton

Surrey

The home of J.G. Ballard, Shepperton is a
strangely normal place on the outskirts of
London. Ringed by motorways and vast
reservoirs yet mainly known for its hidden,
suburban film studios, Shepperton surfaces
again and again in the writing of Ballard and
is as important to his surreal vision as his
childhood spent in Shanghai. Ballard died in
2009 and the blackened net curtains of his
empty house form the central orifice of this
drowning Phantom.

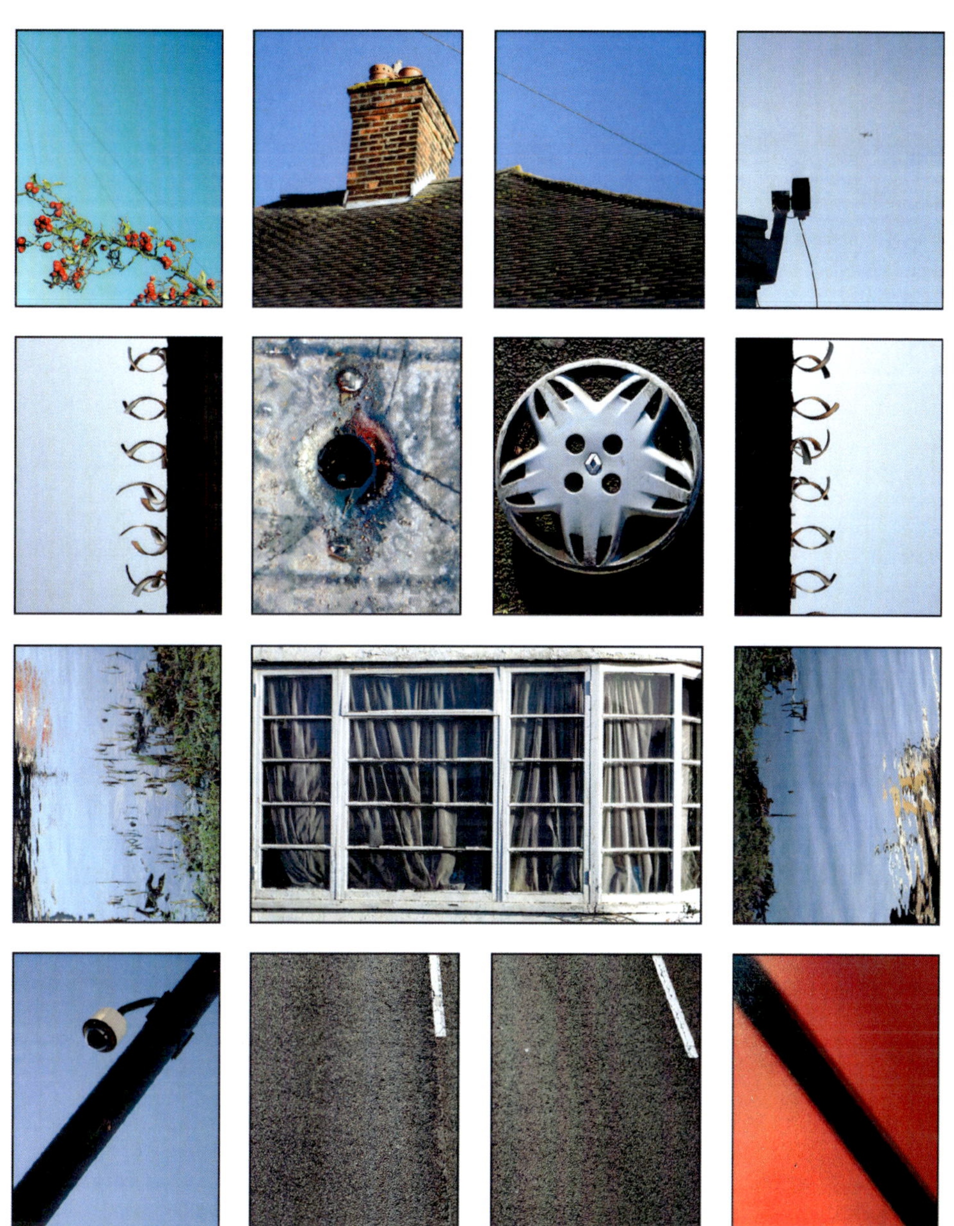

The Phantom of Shepperton (2012)
digital print on aluminum 104 x 84 cm

Cork Street
London

This was where the first exhibtions of works
by Magritte and other continental surrealists
were held at E.L.T. Mesens' London Gallery.

The London gallery was a key site for
British surrealism in the 1930s and from
here Mesens edited *The London Bulletin*
(1938–1940), one of the most important
journals of the English-language Surrealist
movement.

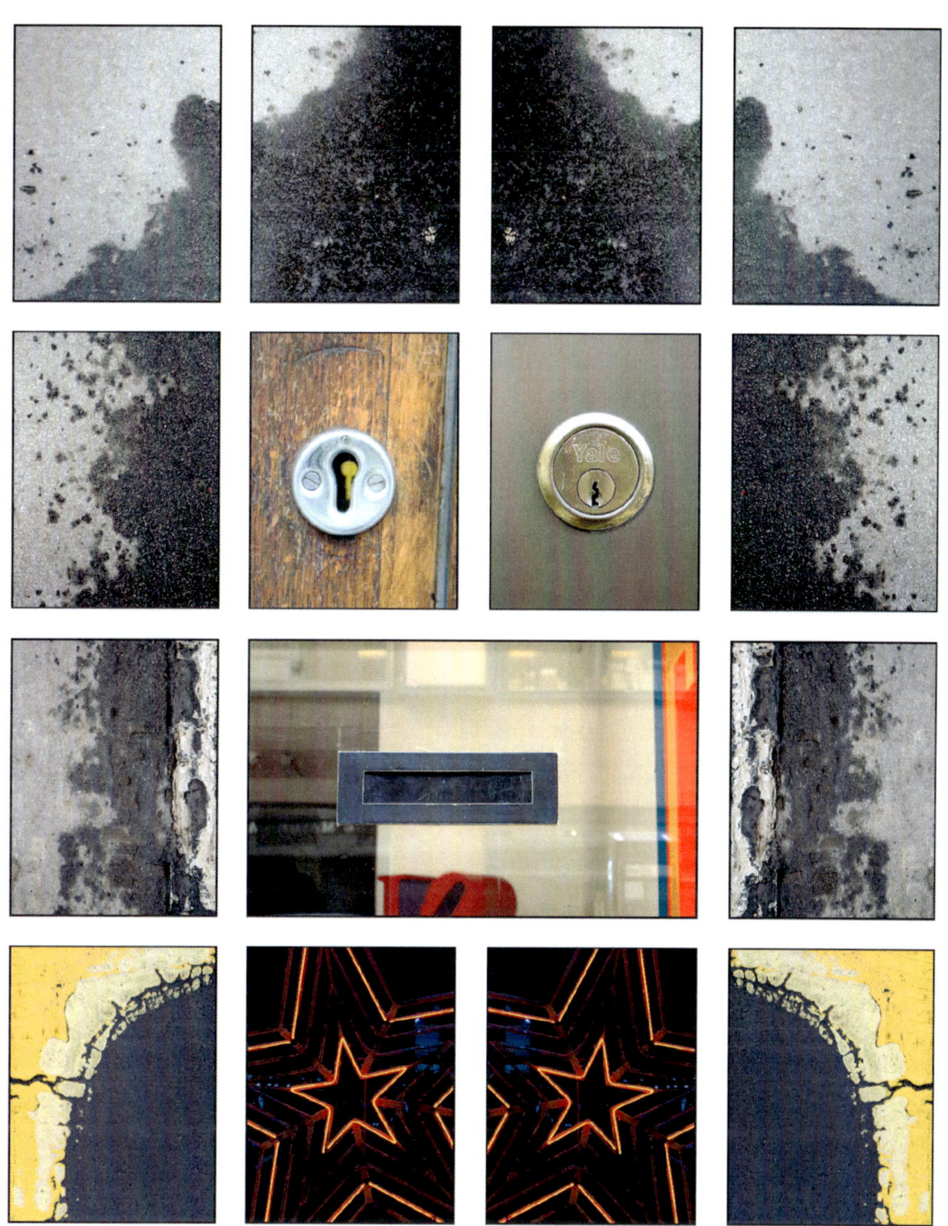

The Phantom of Cork Street (2012)
digital print on aluminum 104 x 84 cm

Maresfield Gardens
London

The Hampstead home of Sigmund Freud.
Freud and his family moved to London after
the Nazi annexation of Austria in 1938. Although Freud, his writings and research were
important factors in the development of
surrealist ideas, the interest was not entirely
mutual. Freud wrote...

"I am not able to clarify for myself what Surrealism is and what it wants. Perhaps I am
not destined to understand it, I who am so
distant from art."

Breton, André. *Communicating Vessels*, Lincoln and London:
The University of Nebraska Press, 1990. (p. 152)

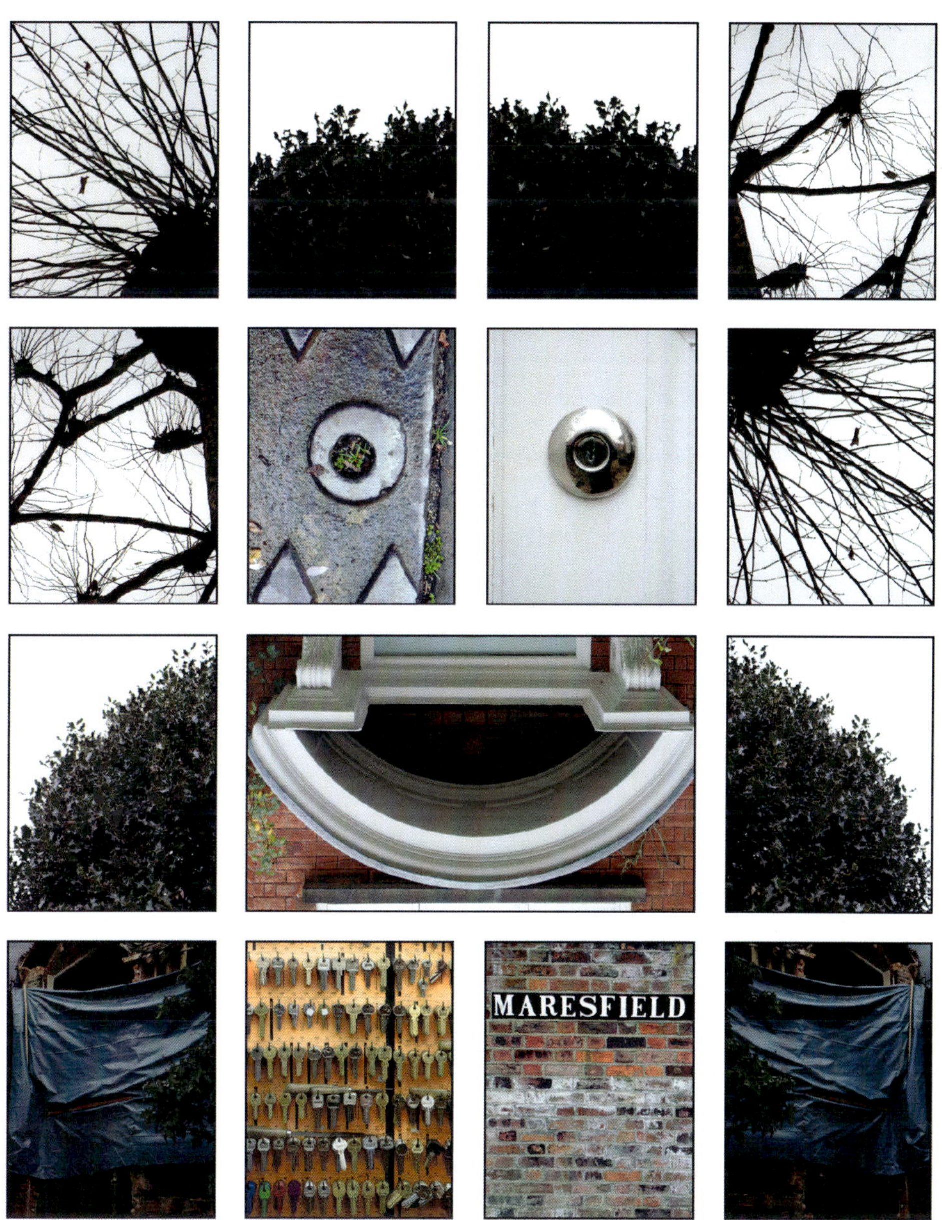

The Freudian Phantom (2012)
digital print on aluminum 104 x 84 cm

Leeds
West Yorkshire

The city of Leeds has a number of connections to the surrealist movement. Henry
Moore was born in Castleford and had close
connections to the city, despite his later distance from the movement he was involved
in the early stages of British surrealism.
Anthony Earnshaw, the *Imp of Surrealism*,
was born in nearby Ilkley and the Leeds
Surrealist Group was formed in 1994 in an
attempt to establish a collective surrealist
presence in Britain.

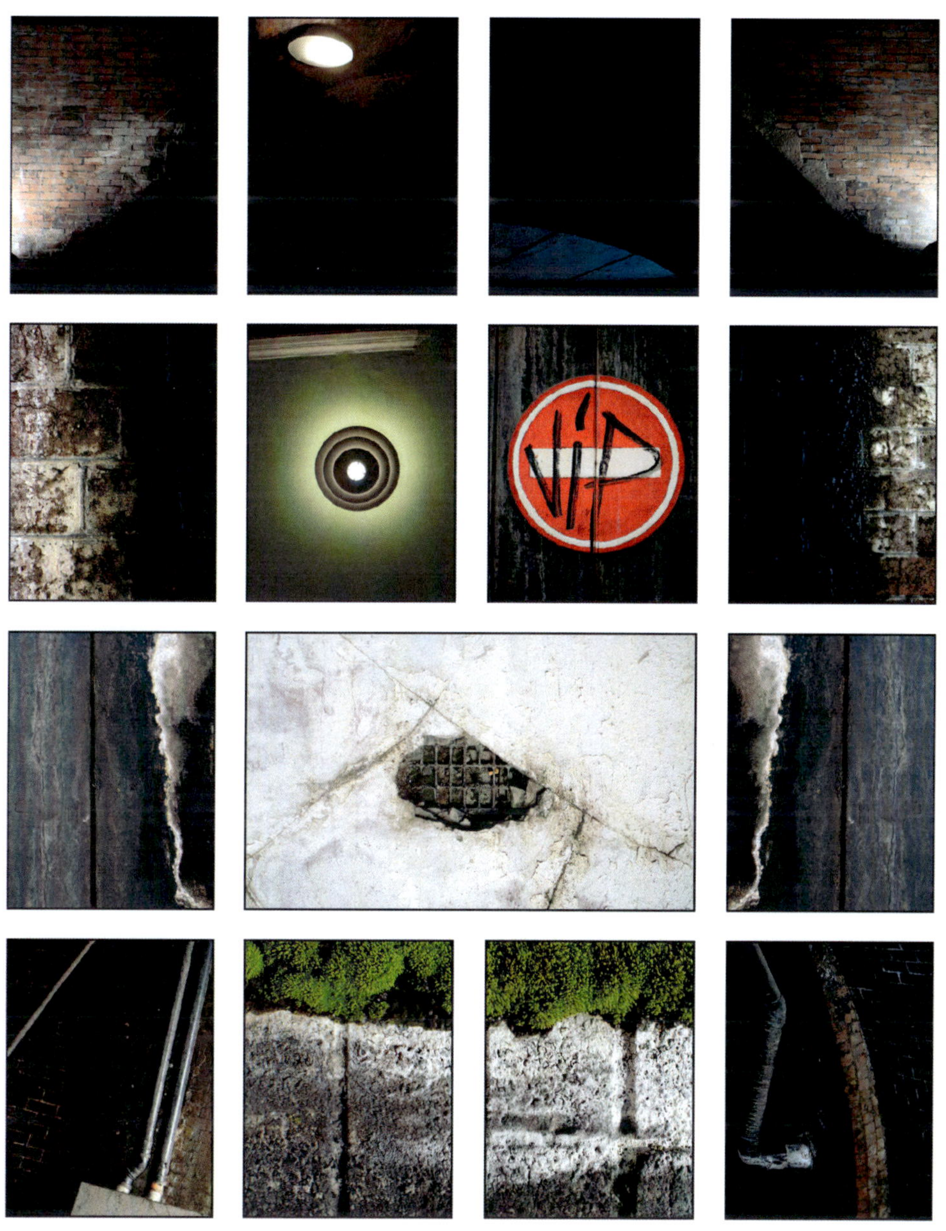

The Phantom of Leeds (2012)
digital print on aluminum 104 x 84 cm

Bolton
Lancashire

Between 1937 and 1938 Humphrey Spender
took over 900 pictures of Bolton as part of
Tom Harrisson and Charles Madge's Mass-
Observation project. For the purpose of the
project, Bolton was named 'Worktown' and
was used to represent a typical British industrial town. Spender was joined at various
times by other artists associated with British
surrealism, the most notable being Humphrey Jennings and Julian Trevelyan.

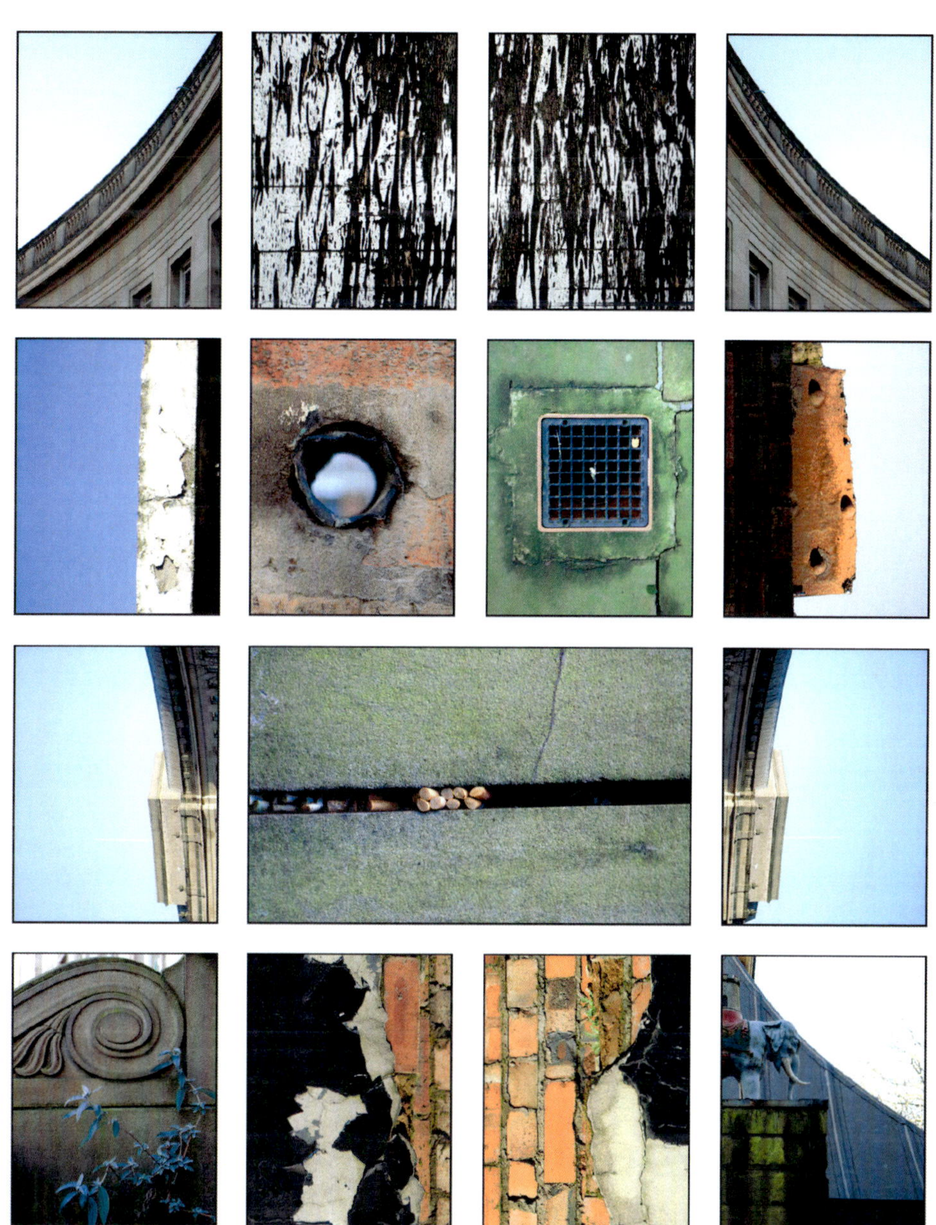

The Phantom of Worktown (2012)
digital print on aluminum 104 x 84 cm

29

Westminster

London

The 1936 London International Surrealist
Exhibition was held in Westminster at the
New Burlington Galleries, Mayfair. It was
through this exhibtion that surrealism was
introduced to the wider British public.

Photographs of Sheila Legge as the *Surrealist
Phantom*, standing in Trafalgar Square, wearing a rose-covered mask and feeding pigeons
on her outstretched arms, appeared in most
national newspapers.

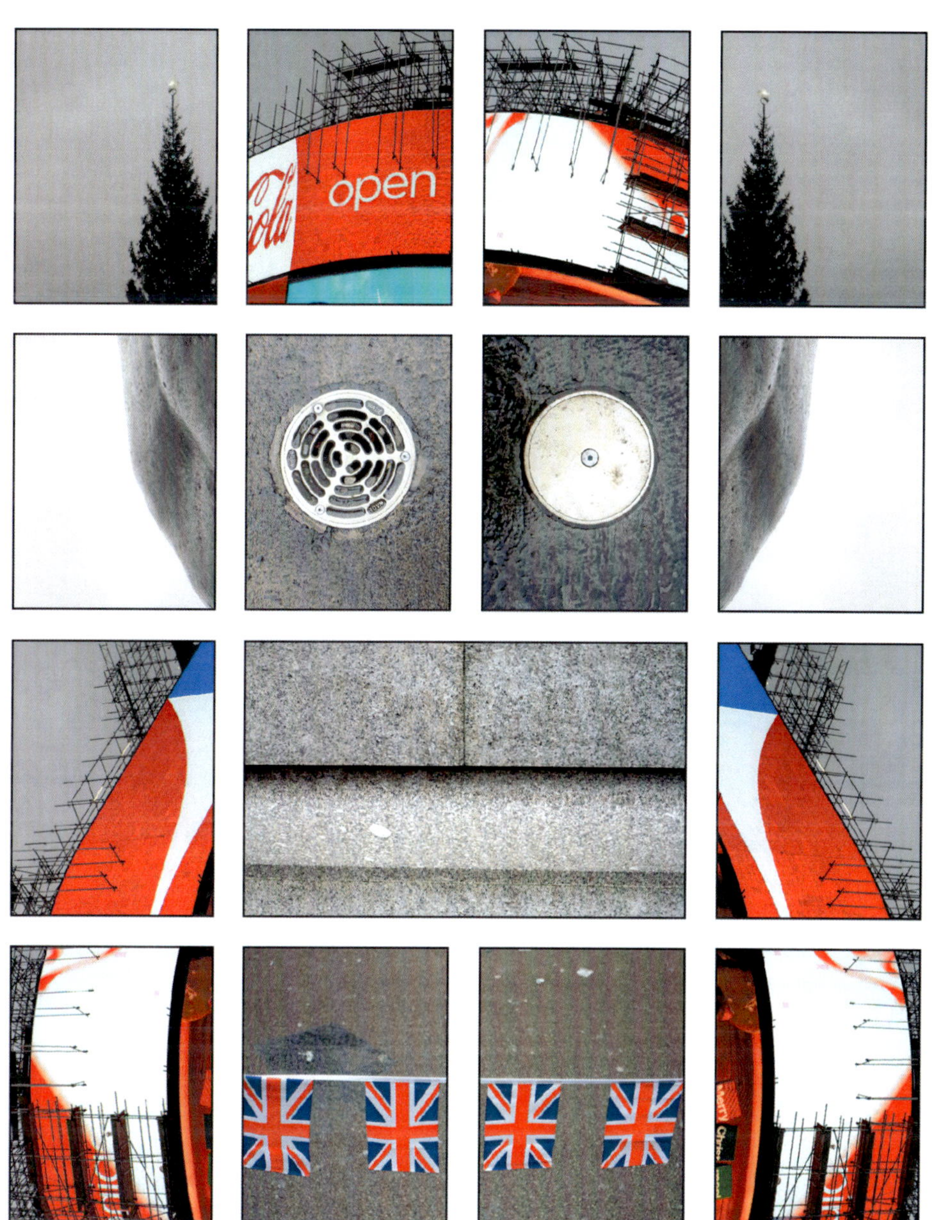

The Phantom of Westminster (2012)
digital print on aluminum 104 x 84 cm

Birmingham
West Midlands

From the 1930s onward, Birmingham
became one of the key centres of surrealist
activity in Britain. Conroy Maddox and
John Melville are the best known of this in-
formal group but other artists such as Emmy
Bridgewater, Edith Rimmington, Oscar
Mellor and Desmond Morris were associated
with the group. They held regular meetings
at the Kardomah Café and the Trocadero
pub in Birmingham city centre as well as
assembling for soirées at Maddox's home in
Balsall Heath.

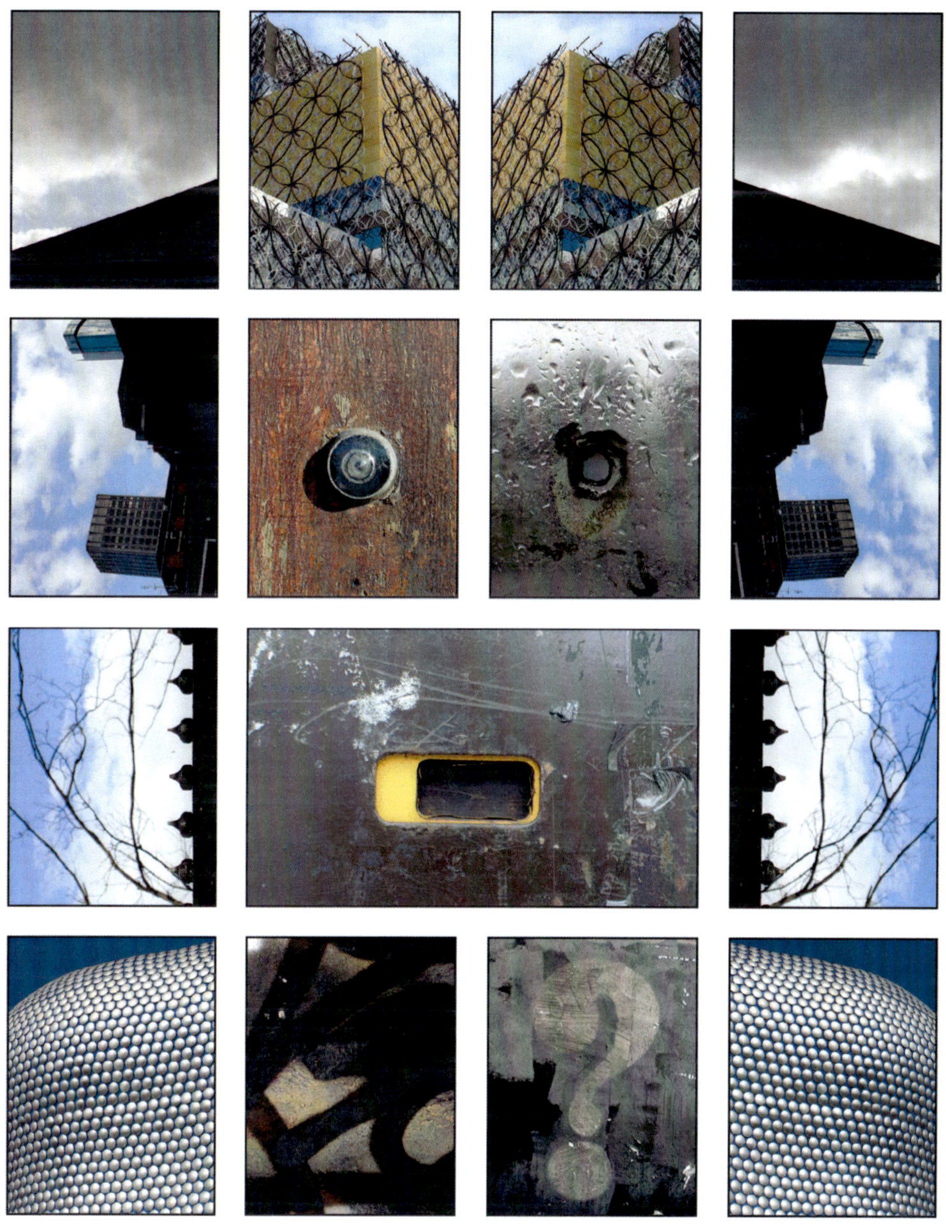

The Phantom of Birmingham (2012)
digital print on aluminum 104 x 84 cm

Dymchurch
Kent

Dymchurch is a small coastal resort in Kent
where Paul Nash painted some well known
seascapes in the 1920s and 1930s. Nash
lived in nearby Rye and, although quite a bit
has been written about his time in Swanage,
he also spent an important period of his
life in Rye. The small town was home to a
thriving modernist community in the interwar years and Nash made the short trip to
Dymchurch regularly. Subsequently artists
such as Derek Jarman have been drawn from
London to this atmospheric stretch of coast
between Dymchurch and Dungeness.

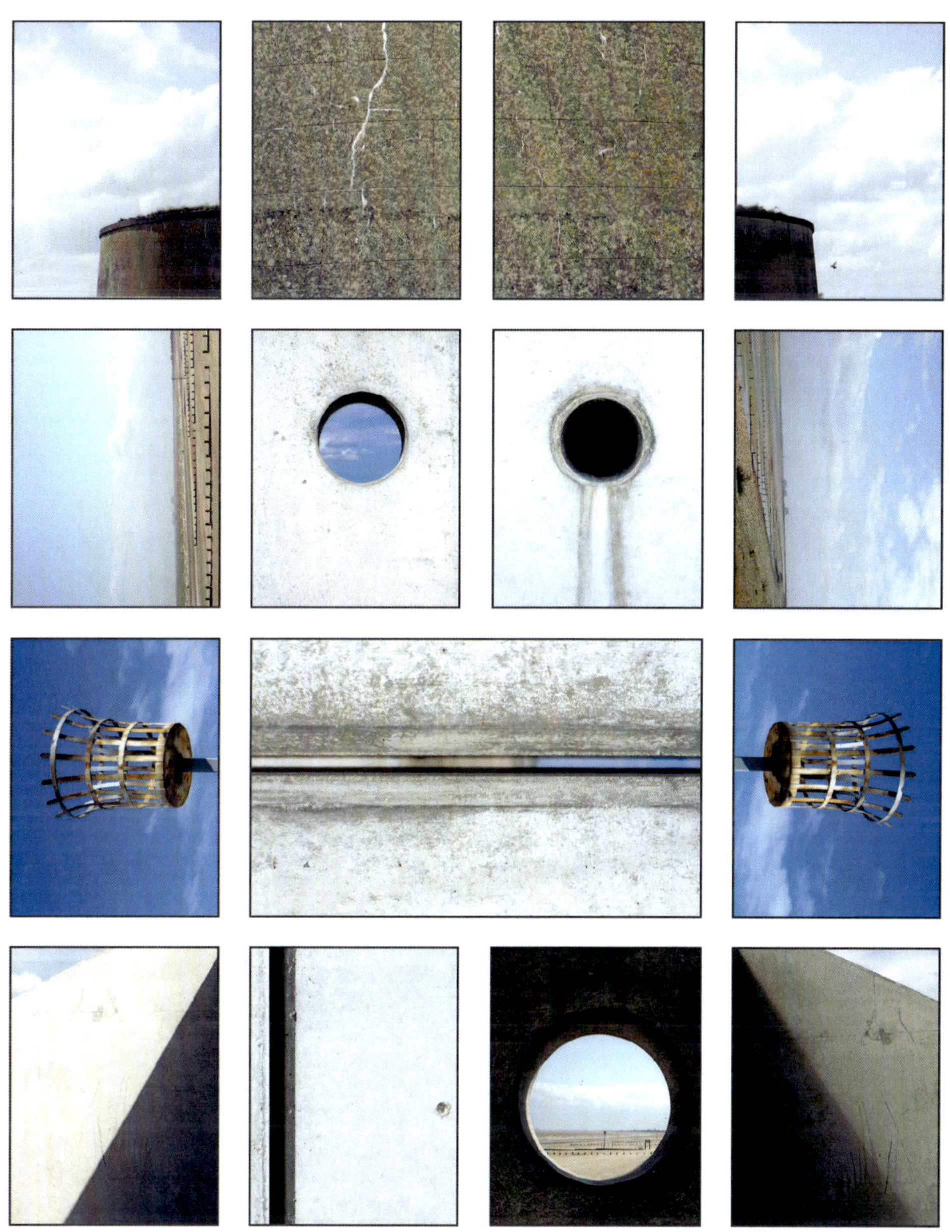

The Phantom of Dymchurch (2012)
digital print on aluminum 104 x 84 cm

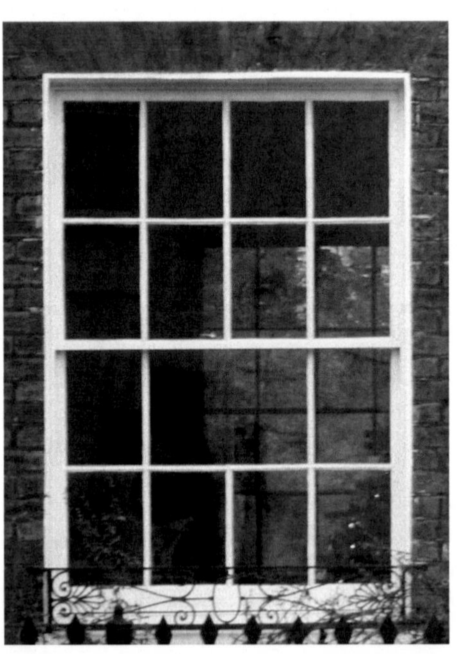

Extracts from the Surreal Phantoms Blog
October 2011 - July 2012
Neil Coombs

The Phantom of Blackheath

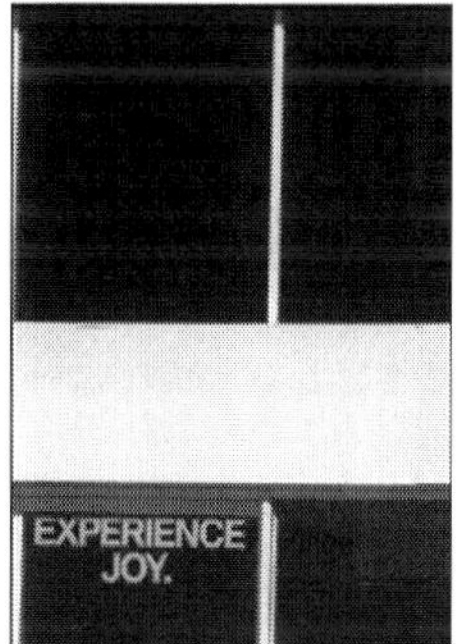

Blackheath in London was the home of the English surrealist Humphrey Jennings for some of the time that he worked at the GPO film unit (which was also based in the village). The Phantom of Blackheath was photographed and constructed in the summer of 2010. During the following summer, riots in London led to an attack on the premises with the slogan 'experience joy' – consequently the window (pictured left) was smashed by rioters shopping with joyful violence.

A Phantom of Nature at the Buttes-Chaumont

During these sordid, phantasmic times, I happen by chance to find myself in damp November Paris where boredom descends in the galleries and arcades and a desire slowly emerges to re- trace the thoughts of Louis Aragon, André Breton and Marcel Noll through the Parc des Buttes-Chaumont.

The Parc des Buttes-Chaumont was commissioned by Napoleon III in 1860 and developed on the site of a gypsum and limestone quarry as part of Baron Haussmann's reconstruction of Paris. The quarry's topography supplied the fabricated garden with its dramatic artificial cliffs and waterfalls and the park is now established with cedar, elm and ash that belie the landscape's industrial origin. In the centre of the kidney-shaped enclosure is a large lake from which emerges a 30 metre rocky outcrop topped by the belvedere of Sybil: a reproduction Corinthian temple from which one can see across Paris to the Zone beyond. The belvedere's island is accessed by a high suspension bridge from whose dizzy heights intoxicated suicides have plunged over the decades.

I enter the Buttes through the point of Aragon's nightcap where Latin-American and Greek revolutionaries meet at the intersection of Avenue Simon Bolivar and Rue Botzaris. Through the twilight drizzle I hear the voices of battling marionettes and venture up the rustic concrete steps, past the Victorian gaslamps, to the brow of a minor mount. The deserted knoll recalls another park – the Hanging Wood of Maryon Park in Charlton – Antonioni's London location for *Blow-Up* (1966) and focus of the infamous lost film of Thatcher's London, *Wart* (1988).

Aragon journeyed to the park one night in 1924 on the suggestion of Breton. They were tired of the cafés and nightclubs of Montparnasse and the notion of the park had conjured in them a mirage that they hoped would lift their black mood. Aragon argued that humanity will perish from an excess of statues and yet, in the Parc des Buttes-Chaumont, the plinths are empty. The concrete cliffs whisper to each other that the statues have fled and, in this desolate darkening, the living people have joined the exodus of statuary.

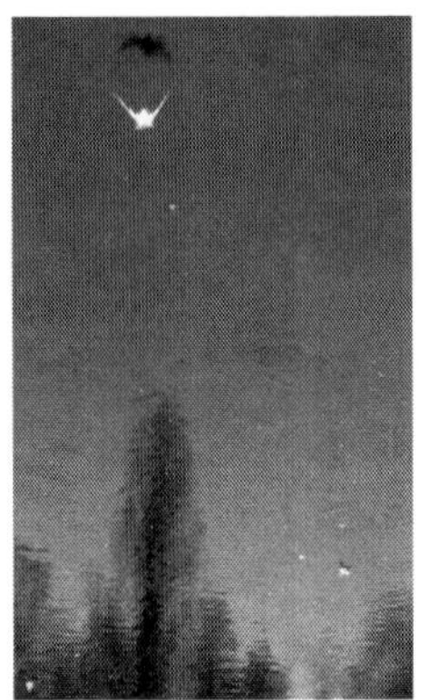

The labyrinthine form of the park's paths draw me towards a higher and deeper disorientation. I am followed by voices, the whispering rocks and battling marionettes take form in hooded figures that pursue me along the suicide's path. They watch me as I photograph the park's appearance, hoping to capture some trace of Aragon's nocturnal wanderings. Tar-macadam cracks below me, drainage pipes to nowhere and concrete logs flush modernity from the constructed world. Facial hedges of over- wrought iron enclose dank, dark passages. I zip my jacket to the top and glance over my shoulder. There is no one in the park and no one ahead on the inky mount, no schoolboys whistling tunes of bridges and sighs emerge from the scrubby hedges or clipped foliage.

I reach the belvedere at dusk and look down across the autumn lake to where the last few souls head out of the park, scuffing over the chalk-stained paths. The wind catches the remaining winter leaves, scattering as sawdust butterflies over the sodden turf. In the distance the steel plate suspension bridge creaks gently. Copper ivy climbs the bronze-stained marble while a fine haze hangs in the cold air. A bird calls "Loplop" to Max Ernst, as it hovers over an inverted world reflected, doubled, in the rip- pling waters of the lake. The limestone path below catches the last pink light of the setting sun as it somehow penetrates the sombre evening for a brief, burning moment. In the misty distance, the Scared Heart of Jesus is shrouded by damp air and encircled by pedlars who hoard hosts of plastic Eiffel towers on steel hoops. Hundreds of multicoloured towers – purple, silver, orange, pink and gold – girdled in order of magnitude. I picture her manacled legs as we gaze up into the eternally open platform, steel elevators penetrate her hollow limbs. The dome of the Sacré Coeur draws back the sky's curtains, I turn my head to the side and the skyline transforms into lips that pout and grin – drawing me back to the belvedere and the wind whispering through the treetops.

Again I search vainly for the phantoms of Aragon and Breton, scanning the landscape for signs of life – ghosts of the twentieth century. The park's voices have quietened and I am left alone on the desolate butte wondering whether I have been locked in for the night or have travelled to a time beyond the Zone. a time that survives in splendid isolation. I take one last glance down towards the empty benches and rustic concrete fences and there, there from the corner of my eye, I glimpse the head of Louis Aragon, emerging momentarily from the tired foliage before vanishing back to a time long before now.

Rockferry Bypass

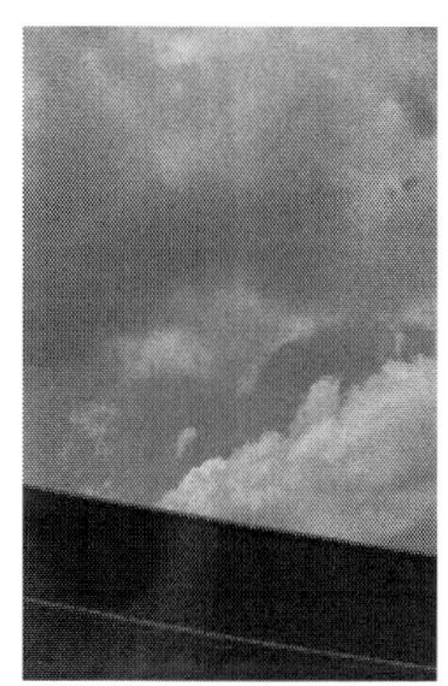

Driving home from Liverpool on Saturday afternoon, I head through the Mersey Tunnel, remembering a *Stranglers* lyric. I hit the Rockferry bypass where the speed limit rises to 50mph, to my right a huge pile of scrap metal looms over a fence, three or four stories high. The pyramid of shredded iron glimmers in the low winter sun. Near the top of the heap the rear end of a Renault Laguna appears to have fallen from the sky and plunged into the nondescript mass of shattered metal – its perfectly formed rear end, complete with number plate and red lights, is buried deep into the mass of fragmented motors.

I laugh out loud, the scrapyard is left behind but I can't shake the image from my mind. I laugh again, manic, I used to drive a Laguna, I've read too much J.G. Ballard – his chromium binnacles embedded in my subconscious. I'm not sure whether the image tickles me as a metaphor or a goal. Is that where I am now – in that entombed automobile? Am

I heading for an end, like all of us, where I am buried in anonymous
pile of analogous humanity? I feel a sudden urge to keep driving to
leave everything and keep heading away knowing that ultimately I will
end up buried in that assemblage of scrap. I feel the empty passenger
seat and imagine a phantom accomplice heading with me, away from
the whole ball of wax – down that road, into that unheard country.

Your Cat

your cat
soaked in milk
its fur matted,
dripping

I glimpse the pink skin
beneath your black fur
I stiffen
I catch my breath

you move slowly
closer
I feel your presence

dripping
melting
into me

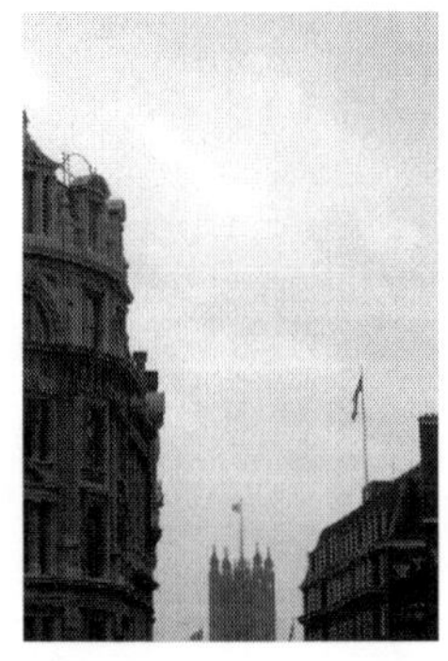

The First Phantom Visitations

After a successful launch party for the new edition of Patricide on
Saturday, I determined to use the rest of the weekend to visit some
locations on the Phantom Map, starting with a trip to central London,
in particular Trafalgar Square. This is the site of one of the most well-
known photographs associated with the first International Surrealist
Exhibition in London in 1936.

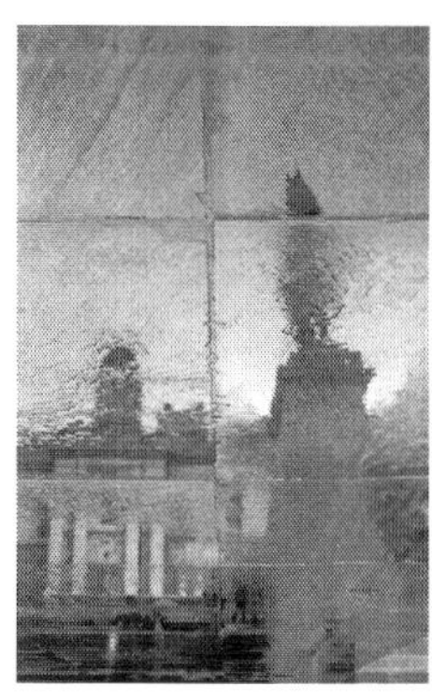

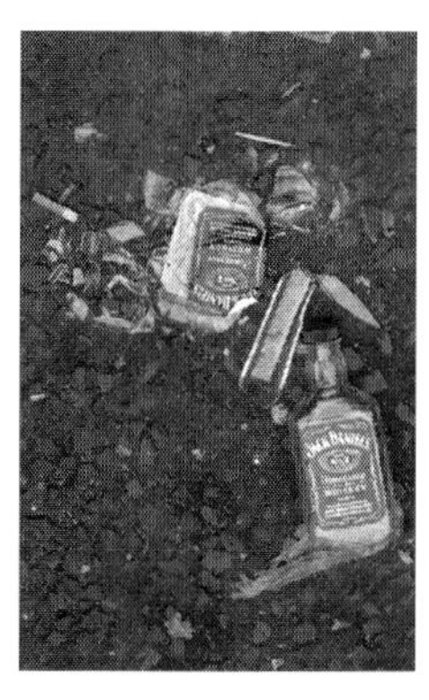

"As the 'Surrealist Phantom' at the 1936 International Surrealist Exhibition in London, Sheila Legge was among the most photographed surrealists of all time. Photos of her standing in Trafalgar Square, her face covered with roses and her outstretched arms bedecked with pigeons, appeared in papers all over England and have been reproduced since in dozens of books."

(Rosemont, P. [1988] Surrealist Women, p. 88)

The day was rather wet and dark but the square was still teeming with tourists, the fountains were illuminated with white light and the wet paving stones reflected the police van parked in the centre by the tall Christmas Tree. The National Gallery looked down at me as I thought of Dame Myra Hess and her wartime piano concertos.

The second stop on the London tour following my visit to Trafalgar square was a short walk up Haymarket, through Picadilly Circus and off to Cork Street. The road was dead with very little sign of life or art. A skip and a crushed bottle of Jack Daniels, some cigarette butts stuck in the pavement's cracks. I struggled to find much of interest on this street where the first shows of works by Magritte and other surrealists were held at E.L.T. Mesen's London Gallery.

Round the corner a queue was forming outside a designer clothes shop - all very dull. I wandered down a back alley halfway up Cork Street and photographed an interesting wall light. I determined to return later in the day when the Empire of Darkness had descended.

Leaving Cork Street behind, I wander up Piccadilly, past the Ritz and hop onto the new Jubilee Line Northwards to Finchley Road. Another salubrious part of London, this time leafy and residential. Large detached houses and established trees line Maresfield Gardens, its red brick homes, churches and other institutions include the London Freud Museum: Sigmund Freud's home from 1938. 20 Maresfield Gardens continued to be the Freud family home until 1982 when Anna Freud, his youngest daughter, died. The building that contains Freud's psychoanalytic couch sits on a road along which his Freud and his patients' phantoms still stroll. I was particularly intrigued by the skeletal winter trees that stood out against the darkening December skyline.

Following an investigation of the environs of the Freud Museum, I explored the intimidating suburban landscape of Hampstead, eventually heading in the direction of Hampstead Heath via Downshire Hill. 21 Downshire Hill was the home of Roland Penrose and Lee Miller and, like the Freud Museum, it is adorned with an English Heritage blue plaque indicating that a surrealist lived here. Penrose and Miller's house is a rather nice three-storey terrace constructed from London Stock brick. Close to a large pub, a church and the Heath, it must have seemed a rather rural and quiet district of London in the 1930s, much less intimidating than Freud's large red brick residence. I took a series of photographs at both locations, following my instinct, I wandered along the quiet streets and through the Heath before heading back to Green Park and Central London in the damp, dark December early evening.

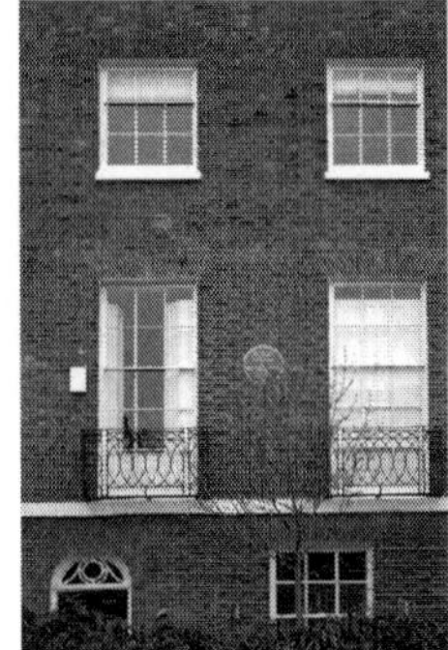

Shrinking Memories and Ballard's Home

After re-visiting Cork Street in the gloomy twilight, I headed off to bed and then, in the cloud of a bright winter morning, I drove west up the A3 along the memories of my teenage journeys in an orange Mini Traveller through Wandsworth, past Roehampton, Wimbledon Common and Tolworth where skinheads once flicked their knives at me on, on to Walton-on-Thames.

Walton-on-Thames town centre; demolished and rebuilt many times, home of Cecil Hepworth and the first cinematic adaptation of *Alice's Adventures in Wonderland*. I parked in the new multi-storey car park that sits on the new Sainsburys and wandered around my childhood memories, shrinking like Alice as I strolled up Bridge Street towards the Rainbow Bookshop (now a café) and the Walton Toy Shop (now an Indian restaurant). I shrink again as I walk past the Walton Hop and the tower blocks from which a fictional *Psychomania* biker threw himself and in which lived pedophile DJs (see *Dark Windows* for more fictional realisations of these documentary tales).

I explored the riverbank and found the clock tower which is all that remains of the Mount Felix Estate – the grounds (now built on) were most likely the location for Hepworth's Alice film. The main estate building was demolished in 1967 and the clock house is now an office block with a car park and razor wire, surrounded by suburban bungalows and apartments. The day was now bright but the ground was sodden, a drowned world surrounded by rivers and reservoirs. I drove across the temporary rusty structure of Walton Bridge and looped around to Shepperton High Street. Shepperton is an even more unassuming town, its quiet high street has a florist, a post office, various charity shops and cafés. Nothing notable, nothing of interest. Turn left at the top of the high street and you walk over the M3 motorway that encloses the town – the motorway to the west, the Thames to the east – flooding and freeways. Walk straight across the traffic lights and you enter Old Charlton Road, a quiet, suburban dead-end. This is the road where J.G. Ballard lived and on which he wrote many of his tales of roads and water, the future and the present, the internal and external life.

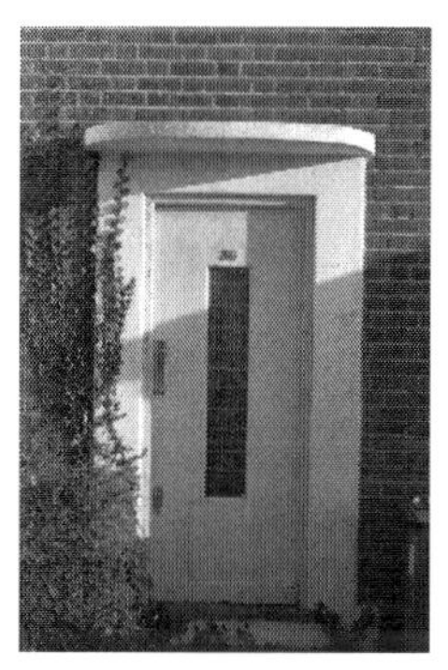

I found Ballard's house with its bright yellow door and dusty windows. Recently sold, the house is being cleared, there are rubble sacks in the drive and a pigeon on the chimney. A young man walks out of the house and I apologise for photographing his home. He doesn't mind. I look in the charity shops of Shepperton, hoping to find objects that once belonged to Ballard – I buy a brown silk Liberty tie and a brown Portmeirion mug for 50p each. The woman in the charity shop has a dog named Toto – she says it is the same breed as Dorothy's dog in MGM's *The Wizard of Oz*. I drive back to North Wales.

The Worktown Phantom

Over the 2011/12 Christmas period I visited Bolton, site of the Mass Observation group's 'Worktown' project. The Mass Observation group was established by Tom Harrison, Charles Madge and Humphrey Jennings as a sort of auto-anthropology and parallels the Parisian *Centrale*

Surréaliste as well as developing out of the 1936 London exhibition (particularly Jennings's subsequent disenchantment with Herbert Read and others). Most of the photographs taken for the Worktown project between 1937 and 1938 were by Humphrey Spender although Jennings also took some images of wet cobbles, graffiti and industrial views. The photographs are held in the collection of Bolton Museum.

I visited Bolton on a beautiful, clear day. The market was crowded with shoppers and Christmas tat as well as barm cakes, pies, fresh meat and fish. The high street was full of pound shops and smokers, there was a great atmosphere and I ate a quality chip butty. The elephants that appear in Jennings's view of Bolton are rightly established in the town centre near the town hall (see Ian Walker's 2007 book *So Exotic, So Homemade* for more on this). Bolton museum has a great aquarium and did have an interesting collection of paintings but has short-sightedly sold some of their works recently. The first-draft phantom of Worktown is a heavy smoker.

Trip to Liverpool

I went on a trip to Liverpool today to re-photograph the Ave Maria door mouth used on the Liverpool Phantom. While there, I saw this job advert posted in a back alley and was tempted to apply. It sounds and looks salubrious....

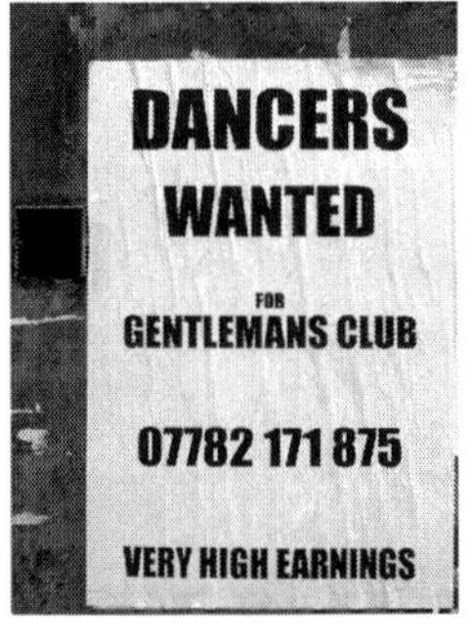

Birmingham Surrealists

I travelled to the Midlands on a wet Saturday in March, taking the early train from Colwyn Bay to Birmingham New Street. My first port of call was the phantom of the Kardomah Café – one of the meeting places of the Birmingham Surrealists from the 1930s to the 1950s. The café is no longer there, replaced by fashion outlets selling overpriced chinese shirts and underwear masquerading as quality outfitting – however one can still see the traces of the Kardomah burnt into the red brick facade.

Although one can no longer drink at the Birmingham Surrealist's

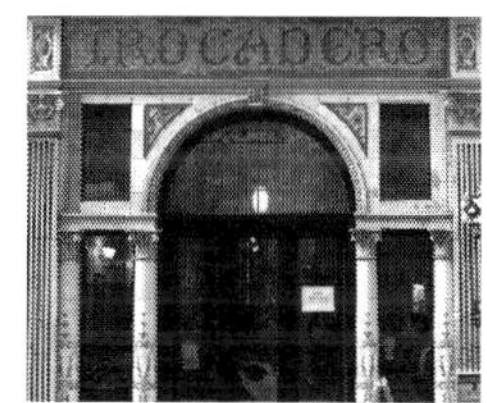

favourite café, the pub that they frequented, The Trocadero, is still open for business. I popped into The Trocadero for a pint of pale ale and some fish and chips and, although the exterior of the pub with its brightly glazed tiles and mosaics has survived, the interior seemed lacking in character. I was expecting a dark gloomy pub with nooks and crannies for artists to hide away and plan the revolution but it was rather bright and open inside. Perhaps the atmosphere was spoiled by the loud Sky Sports blaring through the surround sound system and the wide screen TVs (and by the fact that Arsenal got the winner over Liverpool just as I entered the pub). Maybe it would be better to return one dark winter's night with some fellow conspirators.

However, before my fish and chips, I headed over the the city art gallery to find their small collection of works by the Birmingham Surrealists. There were three works on paper displayed including a drawing by Edith Rimmington that I enjoyed but the highlight was Emmy Bridgewater's "Night Work is About to Commence", a small oil painting that I surreptitiously photographed. Unfortunately there were no Conroy Maddox pictures on display as far as I could see and the gallery staff on duty seemed to have little knowledge of their surrealist collection. I headed out of the town centre and off to Balsall Heath in the hope of finding Conroy Maddox's house where the group used to meet and where I am sure there were many parties. The whole area seems to have been redeveloped in the 1980s and Maddox's road (Varna Road) no longer exists. From the research I carried out using old maps, it seems that the road is now called Hay Park and is a typical dreary street of badly built red-brick houses with bollards and SUVs parked in dull drives. The road reminded me of J.G. Ballard's street in Shepperton: grey, anonymous, suburban, close to a busy main road. The park opposite Hay Park is fairly flat; a pleasant avenue of established trees, some bent football posts and a bridge over the canal. There is one remaining Victorian property on the corner of the park that looks as if it was most likely the park-keeper's home, it is still occupied but the walls are covered with broken glass to keep out intruders.

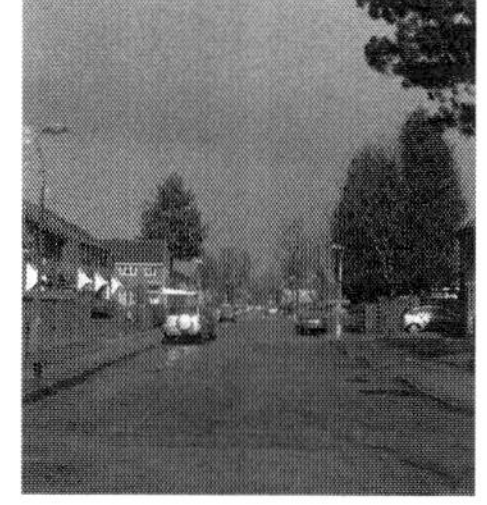

I wandered back into the town centre, past a very interesting record store and many boarded-up shops, dodgy night clubs and garages.

There were a few interesting concrete underpasses and high rise blocks to examine before I found myself back at the Bull Ring market. I explored the city centre, taking more photographs as I went on my way (the Ikon Gallery had a sub-Richard Long display of billboard art that was worthy of a few seconds perusal) and heading back to the Trocadero for one more pale ale before catching the train north to Colwyn Bay.

Sunlight Trip

Today we took a trip to the Lady Lever Art Gallery at Port Sunlight. Port Sunlight is a strangely atmospheric residential estate built by the patrician industrialist William Hesketh Lever for the workers at his Sunlight Soap factory. The estate was started in 1888 and continued to be developed up until the 1930s. Set amongst wooded avenues, there is a peculiar mix of vernacular architecture, manicured lawns and public sculpture. It is hard to imagine capitalist owners of big business constructing such a village for their workers in the present day (if they did it would most likely resemble the fictional Eden Olympia[1]) other examples of the type include Bournville near Birmingham and Saltaire near Bradford. At the centre of the village is the Lady Lever Art Gallery, a great example of the Victorian collector's gallery with some wonderful paintings and objects – where a Roman sculpture stands in one room and a Van Gogh in the next. Chinese snuff bottles, African carvings and pre-Raphaelite paintings all jostle for space in the crowded galleries. We happened to visit on a very sunny March day, shadowy fingers crawled across the manicured lawns to tickle the Lady Lever - I took some pictures and now feel a Phantom of Sunlight emerging.

Yorkshire Phantoms

Just prior to the Easter weekend I headed over to West Yorkshire to see the Anthony Earnshaw exhibition at Cartwright Hall in Bradford. Inspired by my visit to Port Sunlight, I also took the opportunity to visit Saltaire to see another model village built by a Victorian philanthropist/industrialist. Saltaire is now a slightly upmarket residential estate – a world heritage site. The huge Salts Mill that sits on a hill gazing

1. See J.G. Ballard's novel *Super-Cannes* (2000).

46

over toward distant snow-covered moors, is an anomalous architectural artefact that has been reassigned as a huge bookshop cum restaurant cum Hockney gallery etc.…

The compact grid of residential streets with a few boutique shops and public buildings: colleges, churches, hospitals and halls also sits on the hillside with the Canal and railway running below. There is evidence of the more recent past in some of the boarded up shops ripe for re-development and the atmosphere is very different to the world of Port Sunlight.

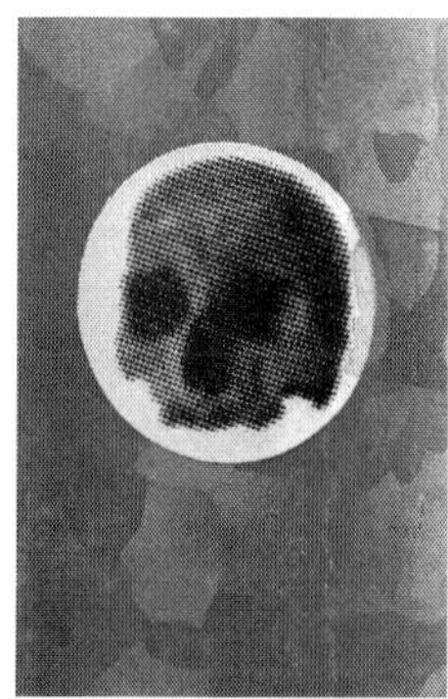

The following day I travelled to Bradford city where George Galloway's Respect Party have just won a seat in Parliament. The deprivation of Bradford has been much discussed in recent days but a visit to Lister Park and Cartwright Hall reveals the historic wealth of Bradford still exists in its civic architecture. Cartwright Hall is a fine example of Northern municipal investment with a small but interesting and varied permanent collection housed in a splendid building. The surrounding park was empty in the sunshine and seemed all the more atmospheric for this unpopulation. The Earnshaw show was very interesting and well worth the visit, I particularly enjoyed the Wokker cartoons and the display of found combs. I photographed the park and buildings, constructing a Phantom from the resulting images over the weekend. The Phantom of Bradford has come to resemble Wokker – most likely a subconscious response to the trip.

Underground Leeds

Yesterday I raced to Leeds along the motorways of Wales and England, hotly pursued by the Olympic torch which was traveling along the road where I live at midday with accompanying corporate spon-sors and police outriders. I arrived in Leeds city centre mid morning and parked underground in a branded disorienting car park burned beneath a hotel. Two men stood at the subterranean barrier and offered me gold token that they said would allow me to leave. I rose from the bowels of the hotel in an elevator that I shared with two sharply suited business-women in high heels who had disembarked from an oversized

white Range Rover and were discussing the day's planned dire deals
with too much enthusiasm. When I reached the City's surface I found
myself in a 21st century shopping mall that led to a 1990s shopping
mall that led to a 1980s shopping mall – I struggled to find my bearings despite having visited Leeds on many occasions before. In one of
the malls I found a long lost stationery shop where I purchased a new
memory card for my camera. I was starting to get confused – not only
about where I was in town but also about which town I was visiting.
The walls of steel seemed confused too.

Eventually I spotted the rear of an older building and wandered down
the street in the warm June sun to find myself somewhere between the
City Museum and the Leeds School of Art. I started to photograph the
walls and doors almost habitually – drawn to the same combinations
of stained walls, victorian masonry and boarded orifices that I seem
to find in every town. As I turned the corner by the main entrance of
the museum, a man came running down the steps and told me that
he'd seen me photographing the masonry and thought that I might be
interested in something. He explained that he was a museum attendant
and ran back up into the building to find a map for me, explaining in
great detail that the map illustrated a tour of the city's stone owls. I de-
cided to have a quick look around the museum which was more interesting architecturally than for its contents. There are some fascinating
displays about collecting and, on the top floor, a temporary exhibition
displaying photographs of Queen Elizabeth II for which there was an
entry charge in excess of two pounds (I didn't visit this display for at
least two reasons). Here is a picture of one of the museum's many ass/
butterfly/quartz displays.

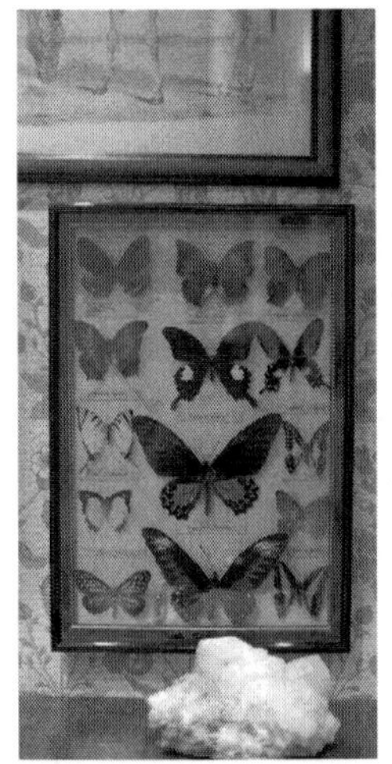

I headed back out and found myself in "Millennium Square" - like
most town centres that I have visited on my Phantom trips, it has
a large television screen fixed to a wall so that people can gather in
public and watch telly in an open piazza – like they do in their living
rooms at home. 24 hour rolling news looks slightly odd however when
the only creatures watching the giant screen are huge golden owls. The
owls were watching a report about a terrible tragedy in Derby. Having
found my bearings, I carried on through town past the remains of

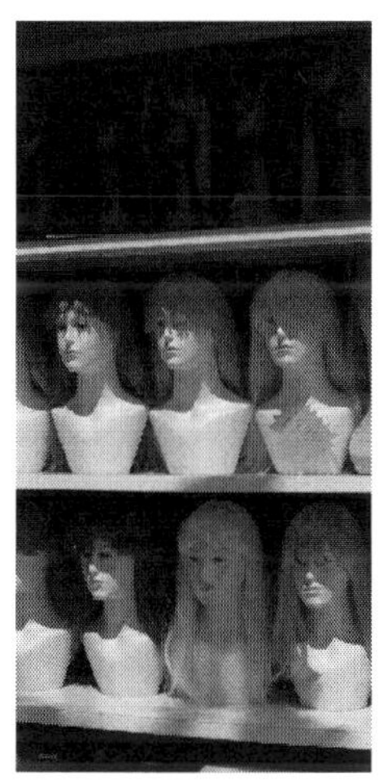

the previous evening's celebrations. I wandered around the business district, past wig shops where human hair is for sale alongside the artificial and through back alleys in the search for an emotional connection with the city. I eventually found that the most atmospheric part of Leeds on the day that I visited was away from the sun and beneath the city's streets. Perhaps it was my subterranean arrival point which drove me back underground, or maybe it was a seed that Bill from the Leeds Surrealist Group had planted in my mind... but I finally wandered under the main railway station where the cars, trains and waterways echo through dark tunnels and under blackened arches. It was here, on the mossy walls and in the reverberating darkness that I found the material for the Phantom of Leeds.

After my wanderings had finished, I met up with Bill in the City Art Gallery and had a very pleasant but all-too-brief chat and cup of tea before racing home again to deal with more mundane matters. On the way back into Wales I passed the Olympic torch – it was heading out of Wales in the direction of Chester, travelling on a vast executive coach with police motorcycle outriders and large police Range Rovers blocking all lanes of the expressway, causing a huge tailback in a Nazi originated tradition sponsored by fast-food chains and soft drinks. I'm not quite sure what the police were protecting.

Alice the Christ Church Phantom

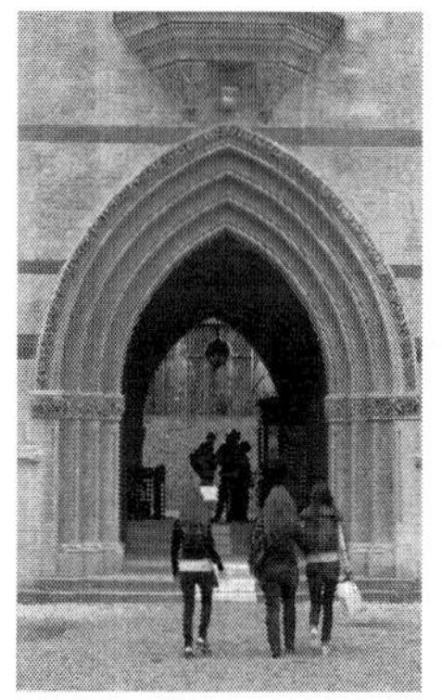

The first leg of my long round trip to examine the phantoms of Southern England took me to Brighton where I was to meet up with Stella Starr and visit Farley Farm in East Sussex. It is a long journey down to Brighton from North Wales – six hours on a good day – so I left at 8.00am and drove at speed along motorways, avoiding the rain. The sun followed me all the way down as I zipped past Birmingham's Spaghetti Junction. As I sped along the M40 I looked up at the gathering clouds and, amongst their amorphous shapes, I saw a figure forming. A wiry, silhouette of a man from the 1930s, his bony, cloudy finger pointing at the distant spires of Oxford. As I was in need of a stop, I felt that I should head into the city centre and try to find the place where Lewis Carroll photographed Alice Liddell against the walls of the Christ Church deanery dressed as a beggar-maid.

I parked in an underground car park and appeared from a dark warren,
like the White Rabbit, into the busy city streets. Completely disorien-
tated, I wandered around following signposts that eventually led me
to Christ Church where the traces of strange rituals lay spread around
the picturesque grounds. Empty bottles of cheap champagne were
scattered around the carefully tended lawns and it appeared that bags
of flour had been thrown around leaving a muddy batter covering the
pathways.

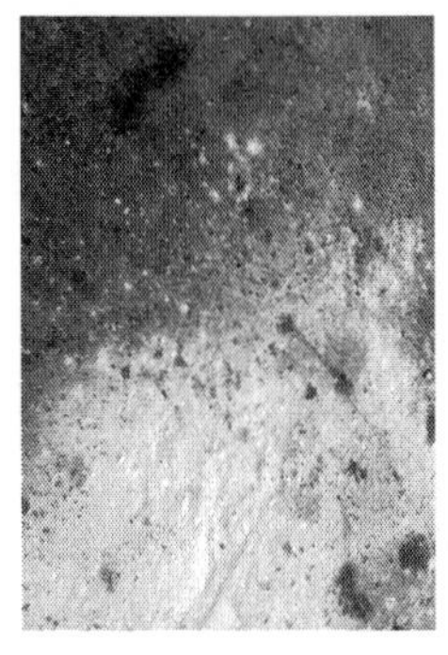

Most of the buildings where Carroll and Liddell circulated were
either closed to the public or charged an entrance fee. The college was
charging a fee of £8.50 to see the interior of the dining room that was
apparently the model for Hogwarts' hall in the Harry Potter books (or
perhaps the films). Some young tourists were buying tickets but I was
short on time and looking for an exterior location – the wall where
Alice and the reverend once interacted.

Searching through some back alleys, I found a tradesman's entrance
that I thought might be an interesting route in but the gates were
locked – the garden beyond looked splendid in the sunlight – unin-
habited and untouched. Perhaps these locked gardens with their ornate
portals were the model for Carroll's gardens in Wonderland. It is said
that the streets of Edinburgh bear the names of characters from Rowling's Potter books and one can see how the small details of the environment can be taken and reconstructed into a fantastical picture forged
by the imagination of the author/artist. The appeal of both Carroll
and Rowling are based on a reconstruction of quite specifically British
elements into a fiction that triggers a reaction in those distant in both
space and time. In the same way that I am searching for phantoms of
surrealism through this project, pilgrims travel to find the inspiration
of works that are meaningful to them – whether it be the location of
a film, the home of a poet or the landscape that inspired a painter.
Perhaps it could be construed as pointless heritage tourism but there is
some alchemy in the pilgrimage and from these journeys, new realities
are constructed. I found a door at Christ Church – a small door that

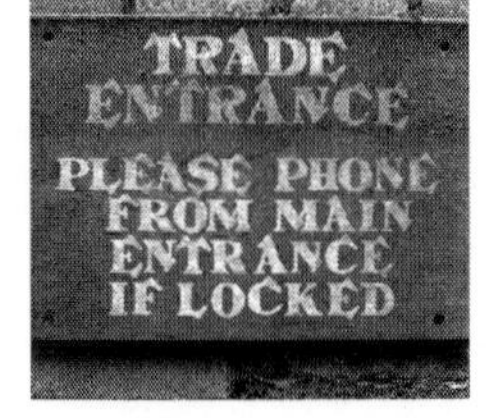

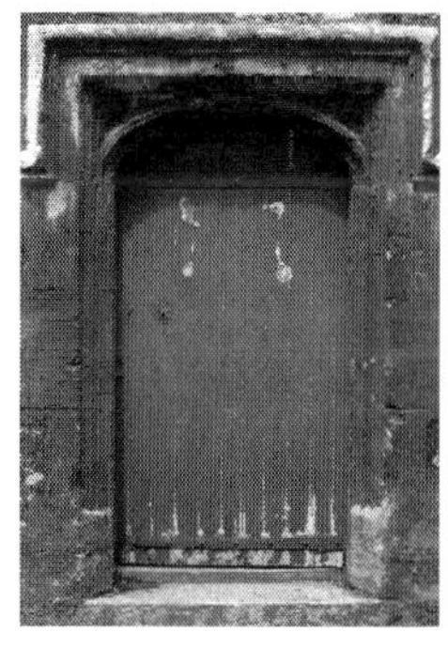

leads to a beautiful garden. The door is locked. There is a garden on the other side. Is this perhaps the garden where the beggar-maid stood – and Carroll with his large camera and glass plate negative stood watching the world inverted by his lens? I had to leave Oxford, I never made it onto the lawn to find the marks left by Carroll's tripod.

Lost in the winding alleys of Oxford, I finally found myself back in the subterranean car park and left the spires far behind as I headed down to the M25. Stuck in a terminal jam around the slowly circulating traffic of the M25. Crawling much slower than walking speed as I passed the junction for Shepperton, I was drawn back into thoughts of Ballard's fictions extracted from his own experience and observation of the nature of reality. Ballard, Carroll, Rowling – worlds apart yet linked through this unresolved pilgrimage. Next stop Sussex.

The Phantoms of Farley Farm

Following my brief stop-over in Oxford, I arrived safely in Brighton on Friday evening which was spent on the borders of Hove supping dry martinis in memory of Luis Buñuel (whose recipe for a perfect dry martini features in his autobiography *My Last Breath* – although there's always the possibility that Jean-Claude Carrière or the League of Toledo invented the recipe but that's a horse of a different colour).

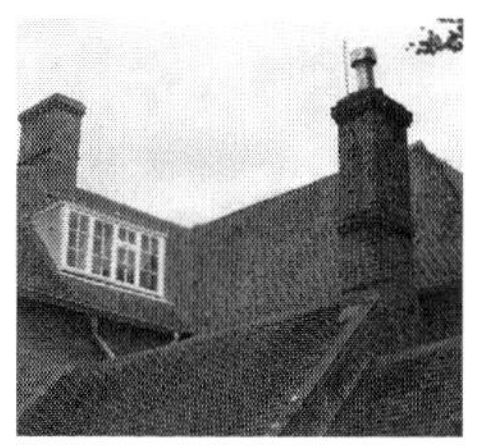

Waking with some trepidation I headed in the direction of Lewes to visit Farley Farm where I had booked a special extended tour led by Antony Penrose. Farley Farm was the post-war home of Roland Penrose and Lee Miller and is known as 'The Home of The Surrealists in England' – it was the country retreat where some of the most well known and influential artists of the 20th century would meet and socialise when in Britain. The house has a wonderful history and is full of the most marvellous examples of art and artefacts relating to surrealism. Much of the Roland Penrose collection can now be found in major museums including the Tate Gallery and the Dean Gallery (now rebranded with the rather ugly corporate title 'Modern Two') in Edinburgh where the Penrose archive is held. Despite the dispersal for safekeeping of some of the more valuable works from Roland Penrose's

magnificent collection of 20th Century art, Farley Farmhouse contains
works that are all the more interesting, not only for their rarity but
also for their situation in a domestic setting with all the accompanying
memories of a family history.

I gave myself plenty of time to get to the farm from Brighton but unfortunately got lost on the winding country roads that lead to Muddles
Green, stumbling rudely into a darkened room as Antony Penrose was
giving a brief introductory lecture on the historical context of Roland
Penrose and Lee Miller, their relationship to each other and to 20th
Century art. A strange scratching, bumping noise was emanating from
somewhere beneath the ancient wooden beams in a hidden corner of
the dark room. I imagined perhaps a large dog turning over in wooden
crate or a cat trying to half-heartedly escape from a timber box. As the
lecture finished and the lights went up I saw that the strange noise was
caused by some large 'guard' tortoises milling about in the far corner of
the room. Antony and his daughter Ami gave a wonderfully intimate
and personal tour of the house, drawing on their own experience of
living at Farley Farm and being amazingly honest about their relationship with their family and the famous visitors. I was expecting a rather
staid National Trust-type tour of a historical building but instead
found myself being shown around a lived-in house where a Picasso tile
sits behind the cooker splashed with bacon fat and where the walls are
covered with works about which Antony and Ami were happy to an-
swer with great engagement, any question that was thrown their way.

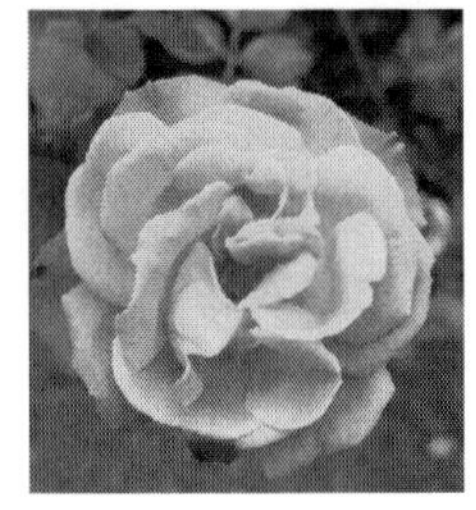

I didn't want to leave the house but the day was bright and the garden
looked inviting in the summer sun. Although I had many questions, I
didn't want to outstay my welcome so I wandered out into the garden
to photograph the views and search for some alchemical traces of
surrealism scattered through the everyday objects in the garden. Some
days later I dreamt of tortoises – like the Freudian 'Wolfman', I had
become a Penrosian 'Tortoiseman' – dreaming of these large shelled
beasts sitting in a strange, leafless tree, staring at me with red tortoise
eyes.

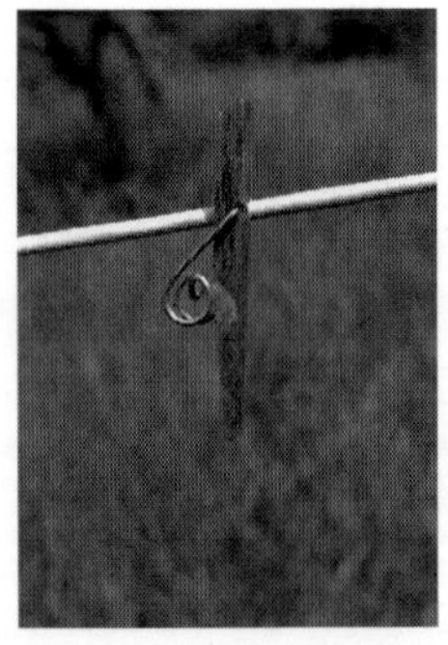

Dym Little Island

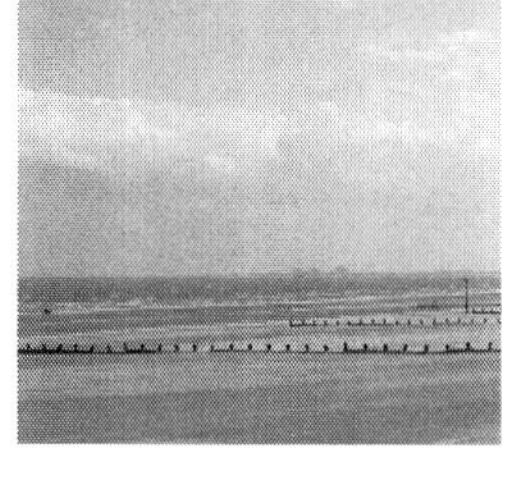

I left Farley Farm on a warm Saturday afternoon and drove along the south coast of England in a general easterly direction. My plan was to stop off at Dymchurch where Paul Nash had painted some well known seascapes in the 1920s and 1930s. He had lived in nearby Rye and, although I know quite a bit has been written about his time in Swanage, I have read very little about his life in Rye. Nash's house in Rye has a blue plaque on the wall and the small town was home to a thriving modernist community in the interwar years. Dymchurch seems to be an inspiration for Nash who returned to it over again to paint the sea wall and, at times, the crashing waves. I had seen Nash's 1923 painting in Leeds City Art Gallery and was surprised at how similar the coast seemed as I stood on the modern sea defences staring west over the deserted beach towards Dungeness nuclear power station.

Despite the summer weekend's warm weather, the coastline that stretched off into the western distance was devoid of any human activity. I had expected to see cycle paths and joggers or children building castles in the sand but there was no-one playing on the beach or tripping along the concrete wall. Maybe the fear of radiation keeps them away or perhaps it never was a popular haunt for fun-seekers. I strolled slowly eastwards along the wall to the village centre, a small agglomeration of 1970s concrete amusement arcades, chip shops, charity shops, 1930s semis and a scattering of older, victorian buildings. From the sea wall you can peer down into the funland below. I dropped down into the village and found a very nice fish and chip shop where I tried a small cod and chips for £4.50 – it was really quite tasty and the seagulls didn't bother me too much as I wandered back along the sea defences towards the car, gazing over the deserted edge of this 'Dym Little Island'. It seemed somehow appropriate to finish my trip at Dymchurch; close to the roots of modernism in Britain and equally near to Folkestone and the channel tunnel that sucks us away into the mainland of Europe. There is something quite Unit One about the concrete sea wall and something quite barren and minimal about the view out to sea across the expanses of sand, I'm not sure if my Phantom of Dymchurch has any personality but I can still taste the chips.

Surreal Phantoms Trading Cards.

A complete set of all 25 trading cards has
been produced in a limited edition first run
of 10 signed and numbered boxes. These
first edition cards are printed in full colour:
9 x 6 cm on 600gsm Mohawk Superfine
paper with a red core. Individual cards have
also been distributed via the Dark Windows
Press.

Here is a special collectors album that lists
all of the Surreal Phantoms for the 2012 -
2013 season.

.

SURREAL ★★★★★ PHANTOMS

TRADING CARDS

COLLECT THE SET

CHECKLIST

- ❏ The Phantom of Celebrity
- ❏ The Phantom of Birmingham
- ❏ The Phantom of Shepperton
- ❏ The Phantom of Worktown
- ❏ The Phantom of Bodelwyddan
- ❏ The Freudian Phantom
- ❏ The Phantom of Plas Newydd
- ❏ The Phantom of Cork Street
- ❏ The Phantom of Hampstead Heath
- ❏ The Phantom of Westminster
- ❏ The Phantom of Edinburgh
- ❏ The Phantom of Saltaire
- ❏ The Phantom of Bradford
- ❏ The Phantom of Blackheath
- ❏ The Phantom of Bury St. Edmunds
- ❏ The Phantom of Buttes Chaumont
- ❏ The Phantom of Dymchurch
- ❏ The Phantom of Farley Farm
- ❏ The Phantom Duke of Lancaster
- ❏ The Phantom of Leeds
- ❏ The Phantom of Liverpool
- ❏ The Phantom of Oxford
- ❏ The Phantom of Portmeirion
- ❏ The Phantom of Sunlight
- ❏ The Phantom of Walton-on-Thames
- ❏ The Phantom of Liberty

WHEN YOU HAVE COLLECTED THE FULL SET OF PHANTOMS JOIN THE PHANTOM CLUB – SEND AN S.A.E. TO DARK WINDOWS PRESS

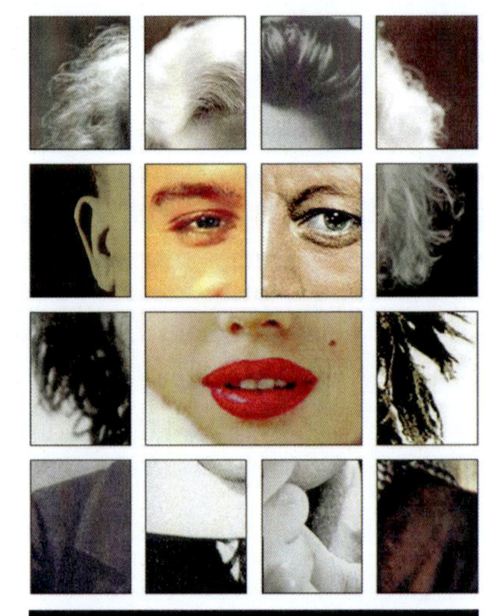

The Phantom of Celebrity
Phantom Power: Einstein, Harlow, Stalin
Hitler, Kennedy, Dylan, Monroe, Presley

1

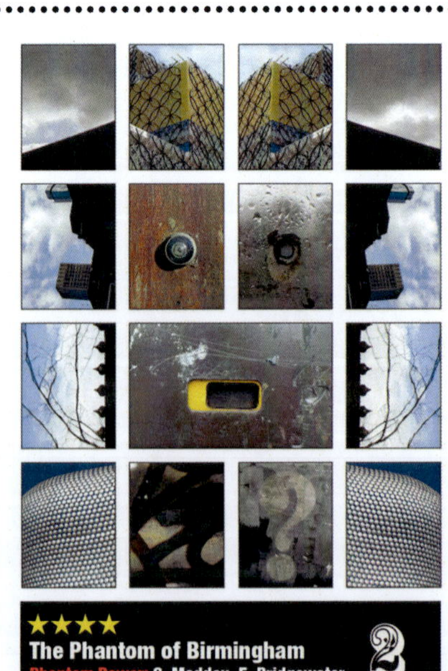

The Phantom of Birmingham
Phantom Power: C. Maddox, E. Bridgewater
J. Melville, D. Morris

2

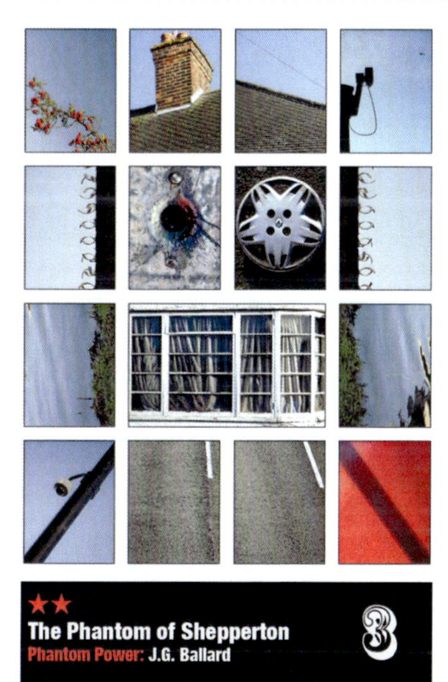

★★
The Phantom of Shepperton
Phantom Power: J.G. Ballard

3

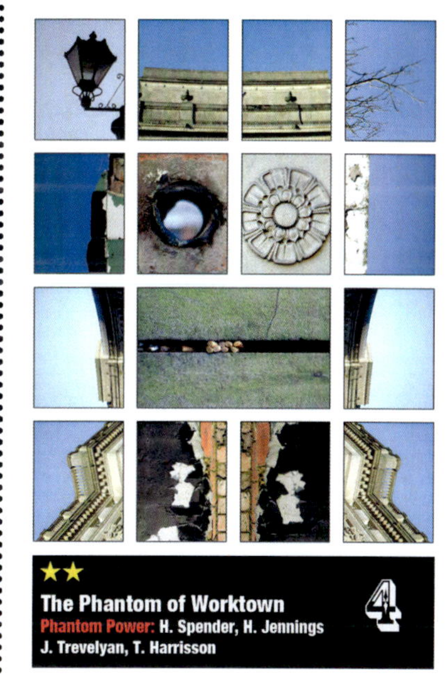

★★
The Phantom of Worktown
Phantom Power: H. Spender, H. Jennings
J. Trevelyan, T. Harrisson

4

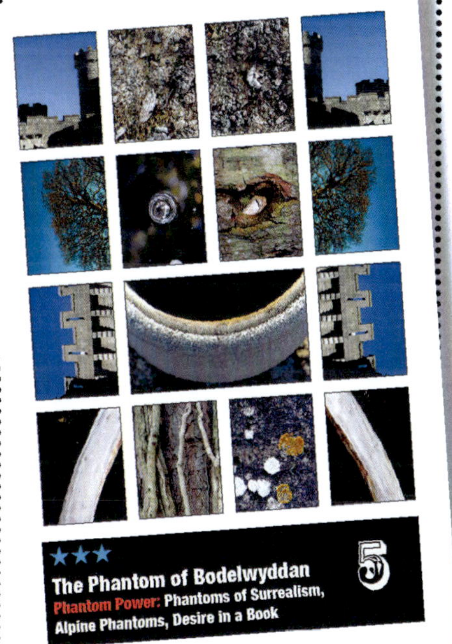

★★★
The Phantom of Bodelwyddan
Phantom Power: Phantoms of Surrealism,
Alpine Phantoms, Desire in a Book

5

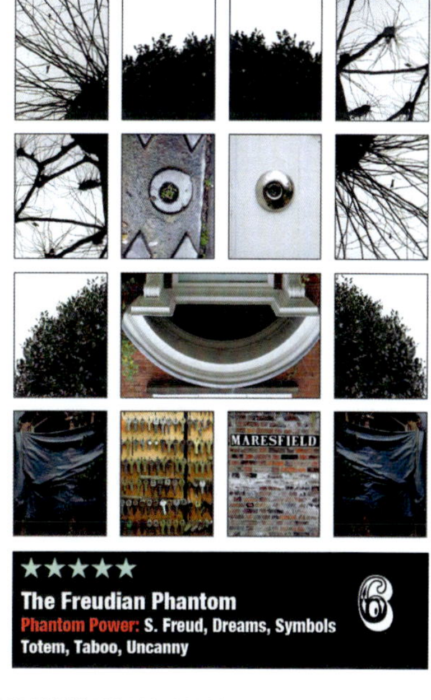

★★★★★
The Freudian Phantom
Phantom Power: S. Freud, Dreams, Symbols
Totem, Taboo, Uncanny

6

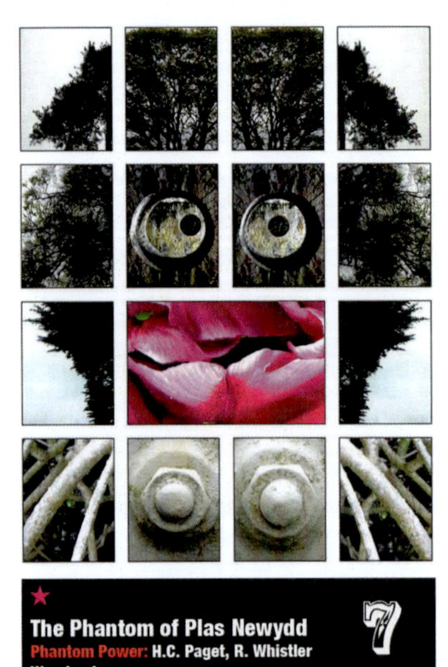

★
The Phantom of Plas Newydd
Phantom Power: H.C. Paget, R. Whistler
Wooden Leg
7

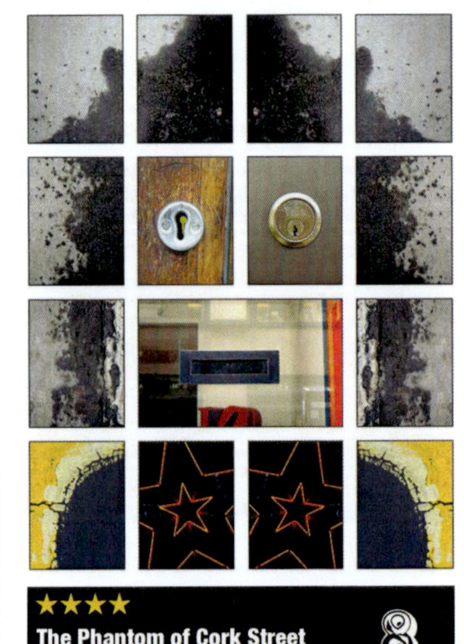

★★★★
The Phantom of Cork Street
Phantom Power: E.L.T. Mesens, R. Magritte,
1936 International Exhibition
8

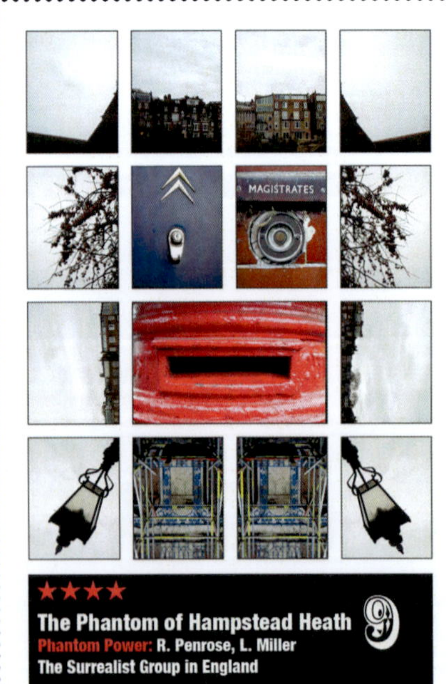

MAGISTRATES
★★★★
The Phantom of Hampstead Heath
Phantom Power: R. Penrose, L. Miller
The Surrealist Group in England
9

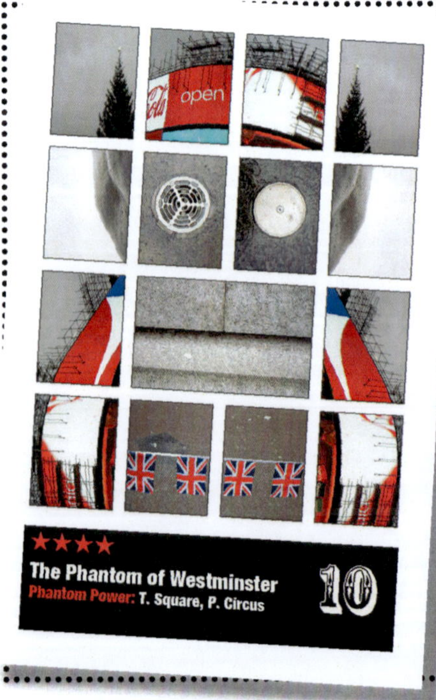

open
★★★★
The Phantom of Westminster
Phantom Power: T. Square, P. Circus
10

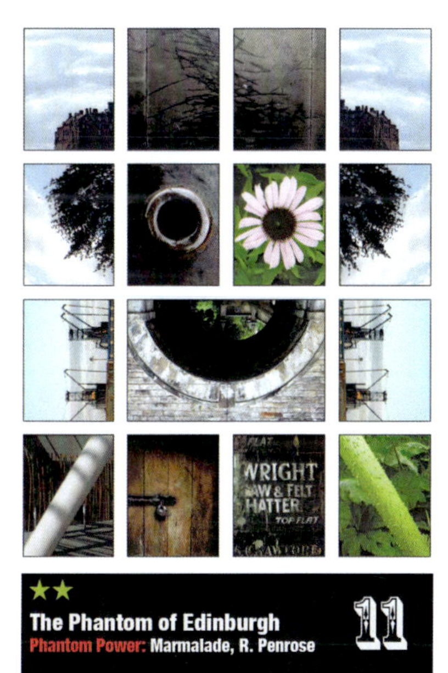

★★
The Phantom of Edinburgh
Phantom Power: Marmalade, R. Penrose
11

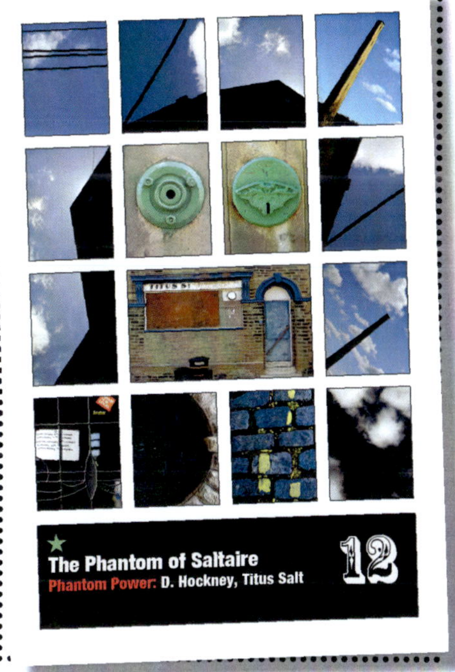

★
The Phantom of Saltaire
Phantom Power: D. Hockney, Titus Salt
12

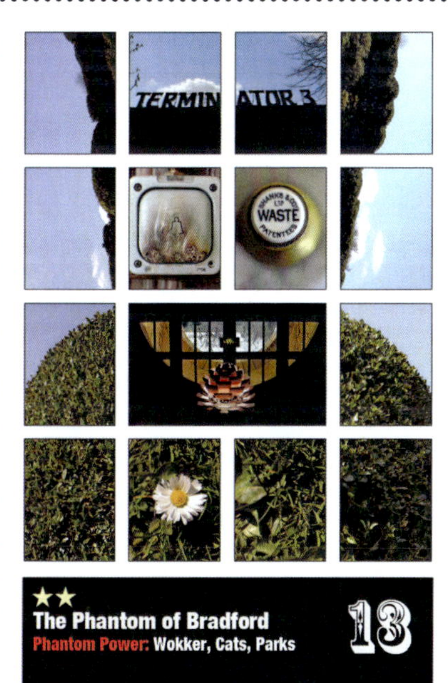

★★
The Phantom of Bradford
Phantom Power: Wokker, Cats, Parks
13

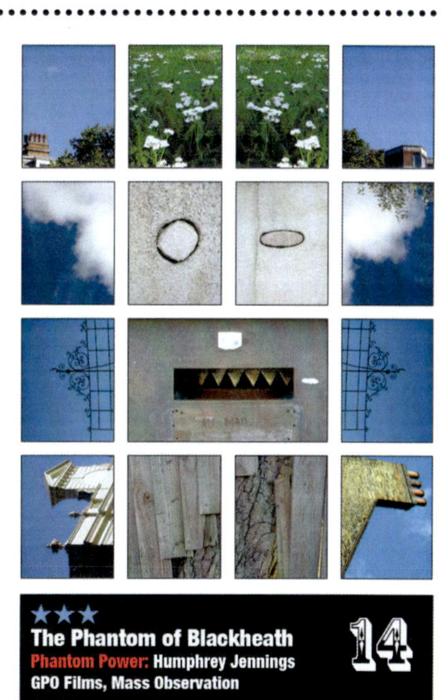

★★★
The Phantom of Blackheath
Phantom Power: Humphrey Jennings
GPO Films, Mass Observation
14

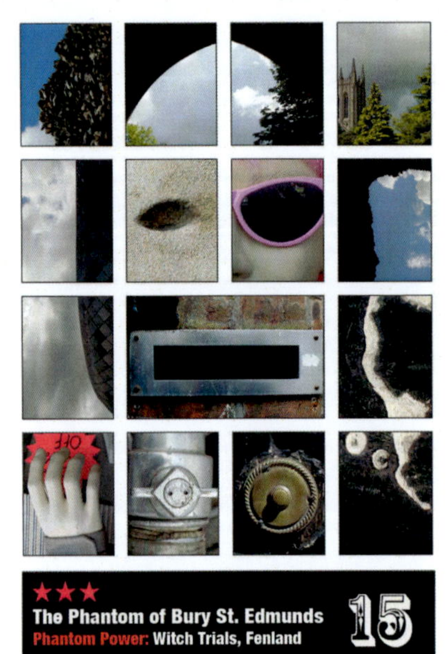

★★★
The Phantom of Bury St. Edmunds **15**
Phantom Power: Witch Trials, Fenland

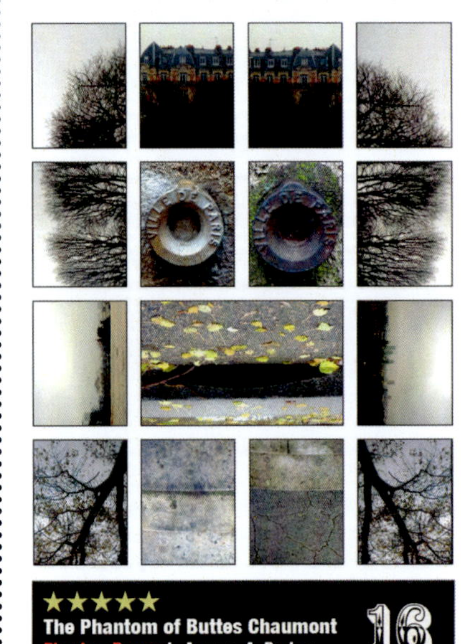

★★★★★
The Phantom of Buttes Chaumont **16**
Phantom Power: L. Aragon, A. Breton, M. Noll

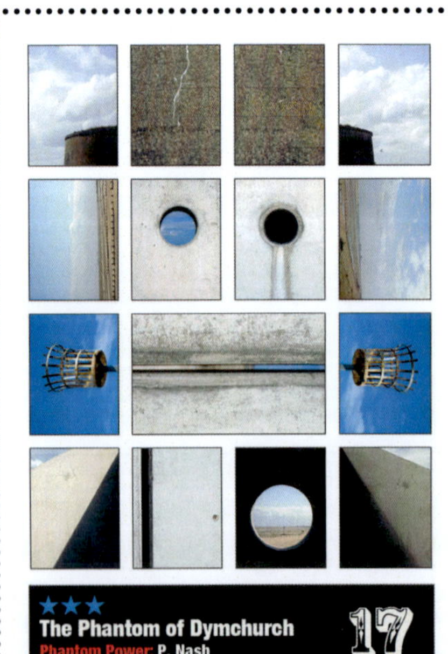

★★★
The Phantom of Dymchurch **17**
Phantom Power: P. Nash

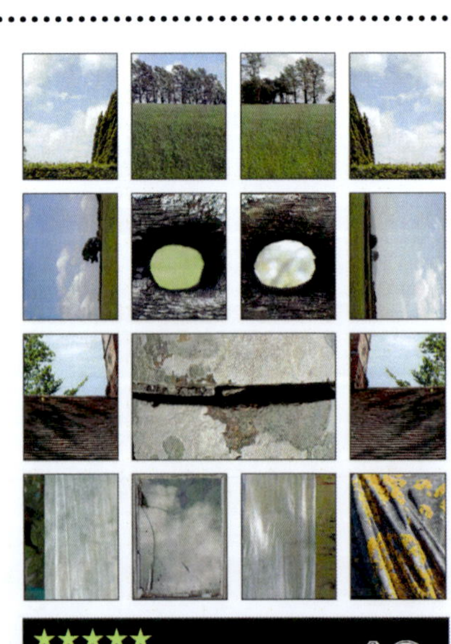

★★★★★
The Phantom of Farley Farm **18**
Phantom Power: R. Penrose, L. Miller P. Picasso, P. Eluard, M. Ernst, D. Tanning

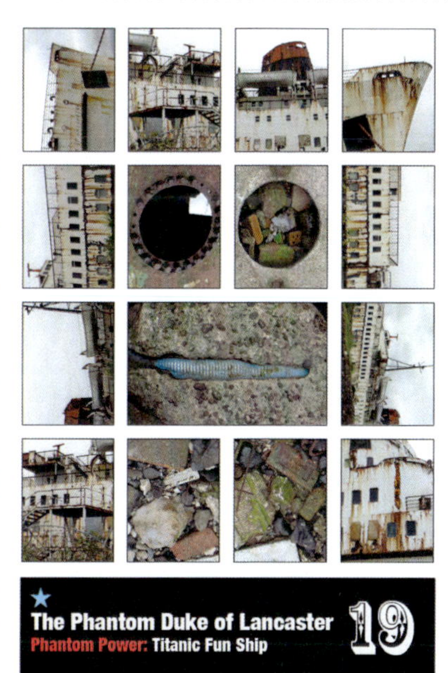

★
The Phantom Duke of Lancaster
Phantom Power: Titanic Fun Ship
19

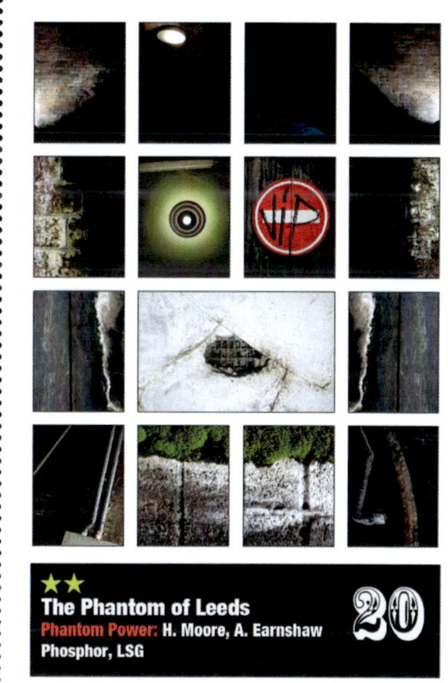

★★
The Phantom of Leeds
Phantom Power: H. Moore, A. Earnshaw
Phosphor, LSG
20

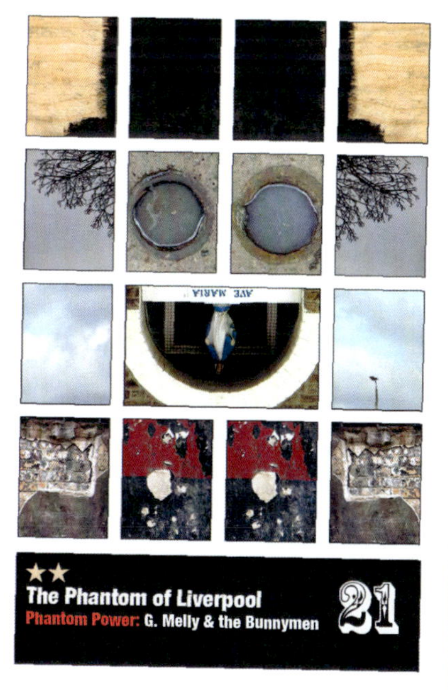

★★
The Phantom of Liverpool
Phantom Power: G. Melly & the Bunnymen
21

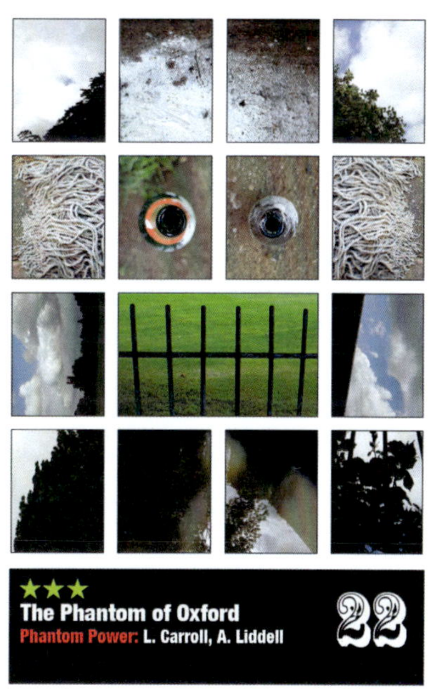

★★★
The Phantom of Oxford
Phantom Power: L. Carroll, A. Liddell
22

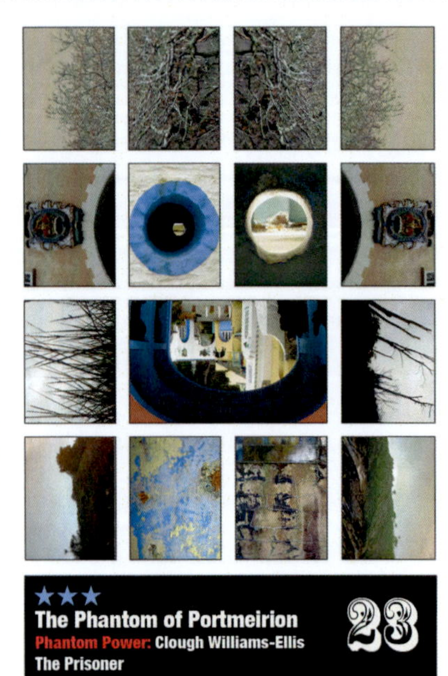

★ ★ ★
The Phantom of Portmeirion
Phantom Power: Clough Williams-Ellis
The Prisoner
23

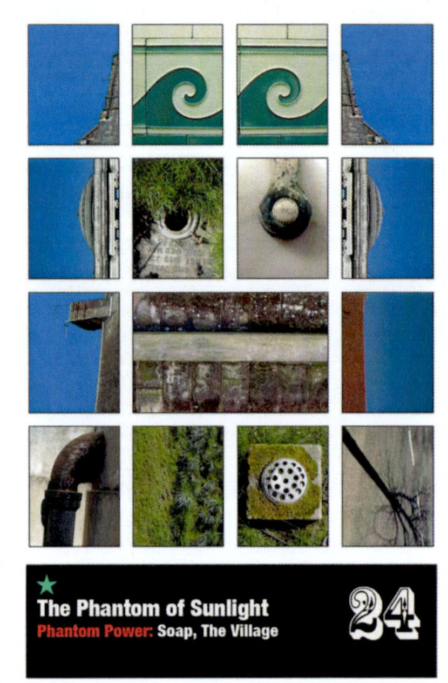

★
The Phantom of Sunlight
Phantom Power: Soap, The Village
24

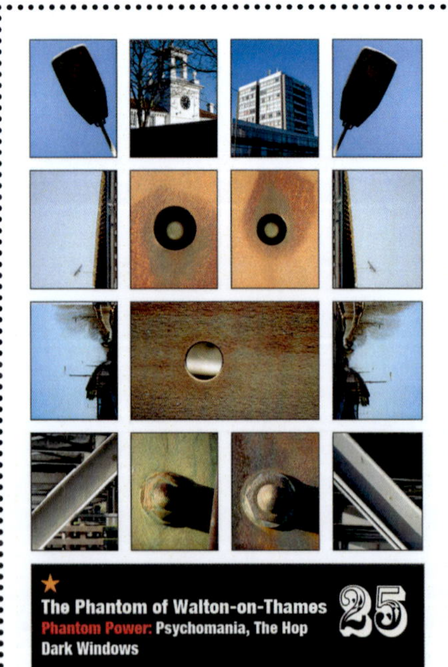

★
The Phantom of Walton-on-Thames
Phantom Power: Psychomania, The Hop
Dark Windows
25

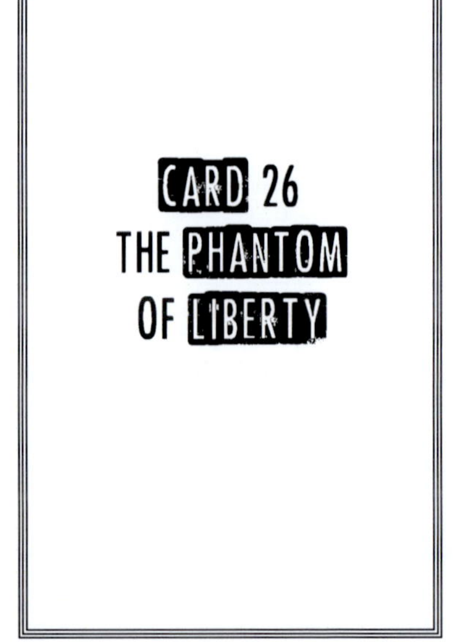

CARD 26
THE PHANTOM
OF LIBERTY

CREATE YOUR OWN PHANTOM
USING THIS SPECIAL CUTOUT
AND COPY TEMPLATE

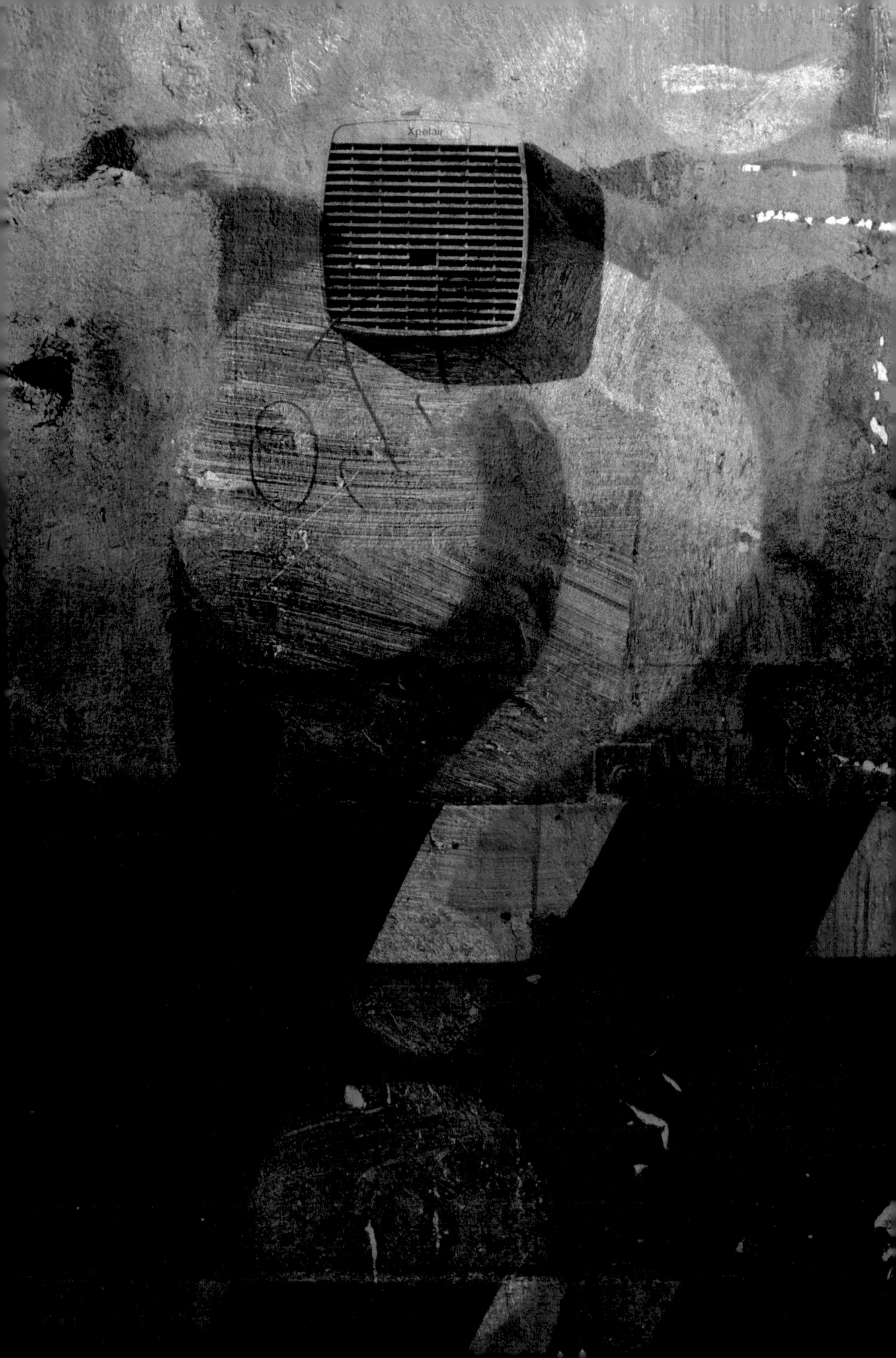

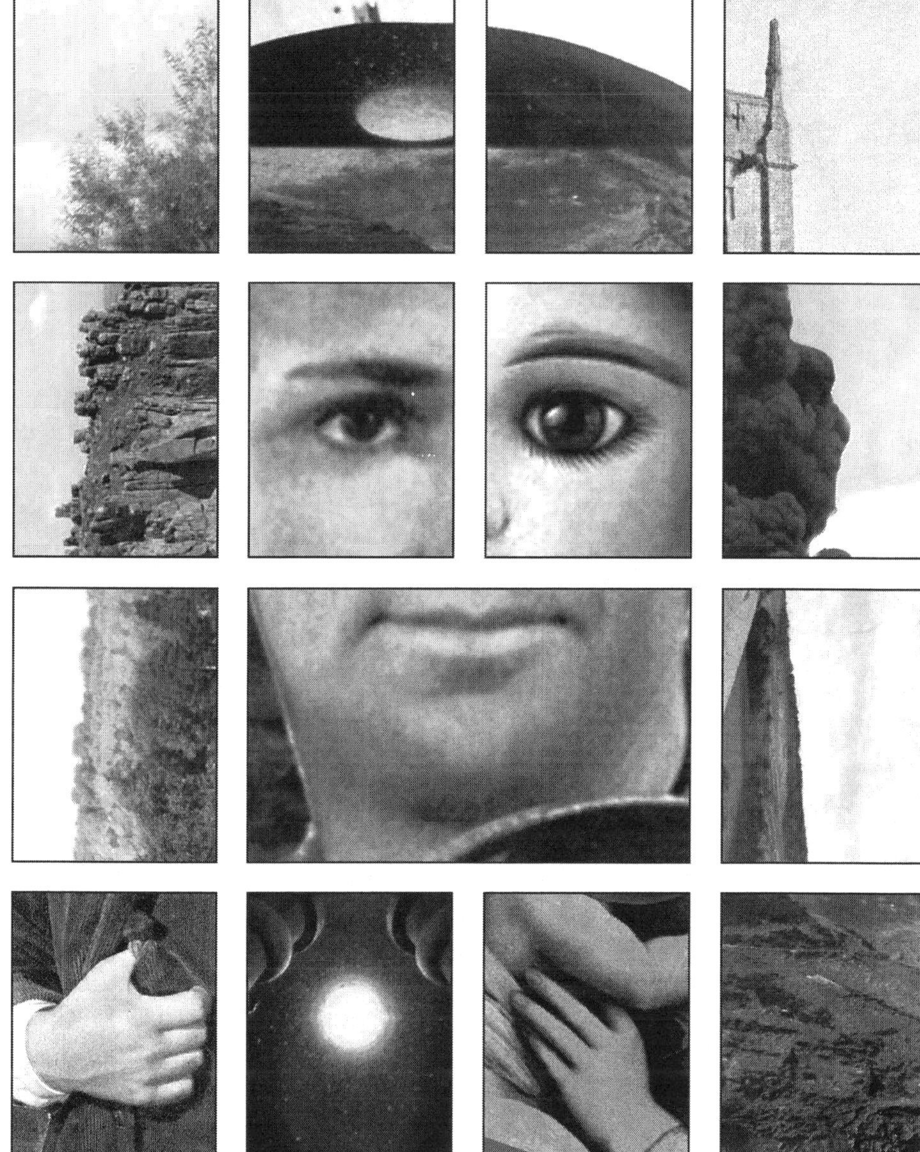

Story Without a Name - for Neil Coombs
Catriona McAra

I have often been enchanted and perturbed by the collage-like dint of apple cheek belonging to one of the characters in *Eine Kleine Nacht-musik* (1943), a small, enigmatic painting by Dorothea Tanning. From this focal point, the child-woman is our avatar, and we see the unfolding scene through her eyes. To the left, her sister's hair seems to grow out of a cracked scalp. There is a subtle disjointedness. There are traces of Victoriana, hints of nineteenth century narrativity and fairy tale uncertainty; an unhappily ever after. We are down the rabbit hole in a hall of doors, speaking to the flowers. The little girls appear to have petrified to porcelain in the presence of a "menacing" motif. The over-sized sunflower is surely the result of the collagist logic but the visual narrative as a whole is impossible to pin down. It provokes interpretation, invites questions but gives no answers. So I forget my credibility and fixate instead on the mesmerising edge of the doll-child's cheek.

Contemplating this at length during the *Alice in Wonderland* exhibition conference at Tate Liverpool, I met Neil Coombs and was soon introduced to his suite of collages, *A Pictorial History of the British Isles* (mostly from 2010). Coombs quickly reveals himself as a latter-day Joseph Cornell,[1] caught up in a productive nostalgia for the materiality of Surrealist practice. The sources of Surrealism, the intellectual heritage picked out by many of the movement's spokesmen, André Breton and Herbert Read, have come full circle as Surrealism itself becomes the intertextual reference point. The modernist art theorist and historian, Hal Foster, labels one of the many coordinates of the Bretonian marvellous as the "outmoded" (1995, 125-6) and this certainty seems to be one of the key principles at work in these collages. Coombs' recent works transport us to the International Surrealism Exhibition at the New Burlington Galleries, London, circa 1936. They also highlight the selective banality of the historical record: the crusades, the revolutions, Charles Darwin's theory of evolution, The Iron Lady's downfall, and Salvador Dalí's notorious diving suit[2] incident are each given equal weight. This comparative action that both trivialises and inflates is a strategy of parody. "Britain" has becomes kitsch, an heirloom to be toyed with, put down and mocked. It is another problematic picture to be cut into cross sections with the kitchen knife.[3] These collages trace an alternative history of the British Isles at a moment when the future of political unity looks increasingly flimsy.

What does it mean to be making quaint collages in the second decade of the twenty-first century? Is this a critical statement? Can the medium still merge two separate realities into an (in-) comprehensible sur-reality? Is the work lost in reverie or does it persuasively re-present and pinpoint a more accurate history of Surrealism than any of the recapitulations offered by contemporary scholarship that refuses to dress-up or practice what it preaches? The home-made nostalgia is both poignant and anachronistic in an era of digital manipulation where "cut and paste" shorthand is taken for granted. The escapism offered by an analogue tactility or colloquial clutter has become deeply appeal-ing. Ephemera has turned into a collectable substitute for a bygone era. It is both retro and deeply niche. For, in the clinical vacuum of today's "paper-free" office, the marvellous can only be re-invoked by the lost dog-eared corner and the infra-thin of the scissor-snip.

The Surrealist doll makes her triumphant reappearance throughout Coombs' collages. She is a persistent memory, an inherited sense of Victoriana sharpened by the historical caesura of play between now and then. This time *La poupée* is the culprit[4] – whether committing random acts of pyromania, devouring the art critic or inconspicuously fleeing the scene of the crime, butter simply wouldn't melt on this maniacal doll-face. Perpetrators in porcelain. Perturbation, my sister's sister's sister![5] For goodness sake, try to remember what happened to Meret Oppenheim's governess![6] Like the game of *cadavre exquis*, the doll has become another Surrealist cliché or dead metaphor to be tripped over, and here her legs are lurking.

The Death of Thatcherism in Britannia presents a cunning visual pun which conflates 80's yuppiedom with the pastoral pursuit of roof thatching. Here a giant feminine leg bursts forth Alice-like, and the recycled myth of Britannia (as an ancient Roman name for Great Britain, colonial emblem, and stand-in for a certain conservative prime minister), is triply twisted into an ironic statement. In *The Final Proof of Inferiority* the true dilemma of the water-bound fortress and the foolishness of the aristocracy are revealed using a combination of the Lilliputian, Laputian and Brobdingnagian visual languages of Jonathan Swift.

In conclusion, the "Coombsian collage" is informed by Surrealism as his chief source of inspiration, and used to make an effective visual commentary about the state of play in contemporary culture and politics, whilst exposing the short-sighted understanding of the past. From the inside of the castle, the spectres of these collages haunt the imagination. However, one must remember that these are not our childhoods that are being re-presented here. They are a Surrealist's memories that are being borrowed in order, to quote Foster's second-hand formulation of Breton, to "re-enchant a disenchanted world".

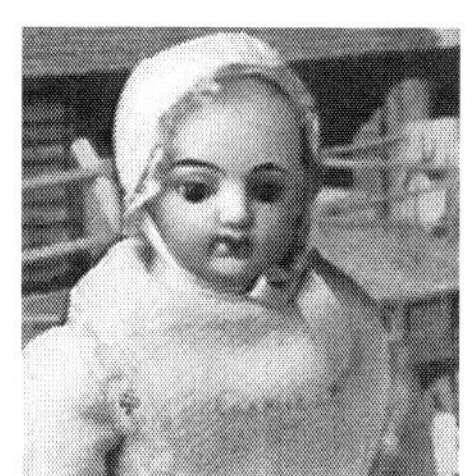

Works Cited: Foster, Hal. *Compulsive Beauty*, Cambridge and London: The MIT Press, 1995. (p. 19)

1. The title of my short essay is a reference to Cornell's series of collage-homages, *Story Without a Name – for Max Ernst* (1942).
2. As the story goes, Salvador Dalí attempted to give a lecture whilst wearing a diving suit at the International Surrealism Exhibition in London but quickly ran out of air and had to be rescued.
3. See Hannah Höch's photomontage, *Cut with the Kitchen Knife: Weimar Through the Last Beer-Belly Cultural Epoch of Germany* (1919).
4. See Hans Bellmer's series of *Dolls* from the 1930s in various media.
5. An exaggerated formulation of one of Max Ernst's collage novel characters, Perturbation, my sister, from *La femme 100 têtes* (1929).
6. See Meret Oppenheim's assisted readymade *My Nurse, Ma Gouvernante, Mein Kindermädchen* (1936).

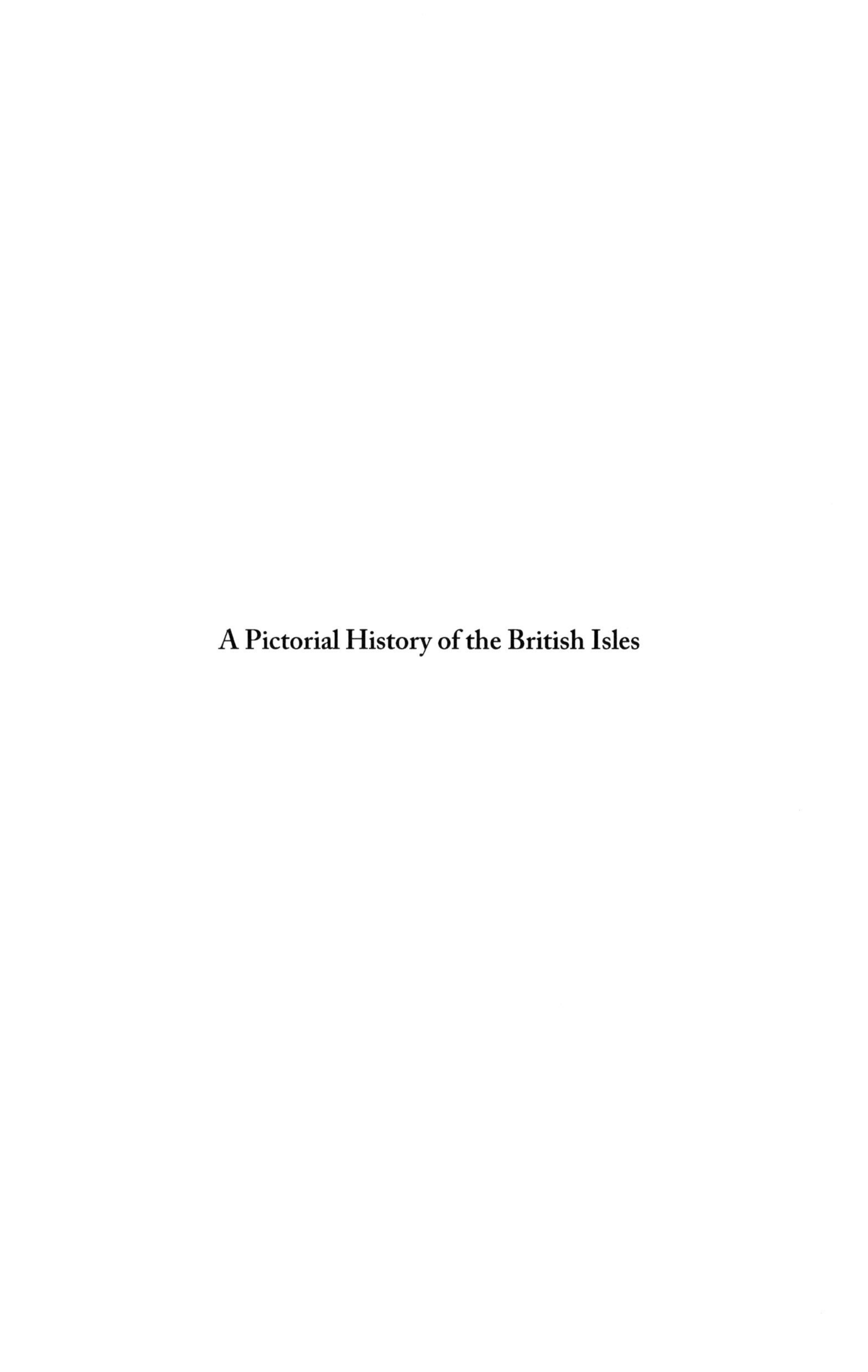

A Pictorial History of the British Isles

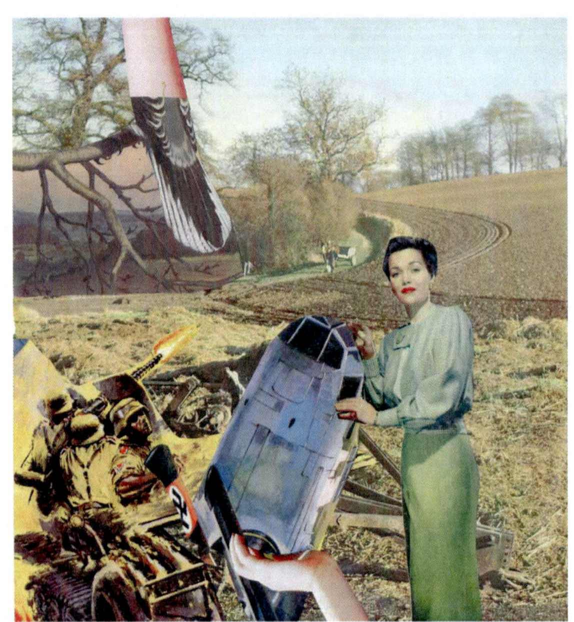

Above:
Buried in the Landscape of History (2010)
collage 27 x 26 cm

Opposite:
*The Tragic Demise of Dali at the London
International Surrealist Exhibition* (2010)
collage 27 x 26 cm

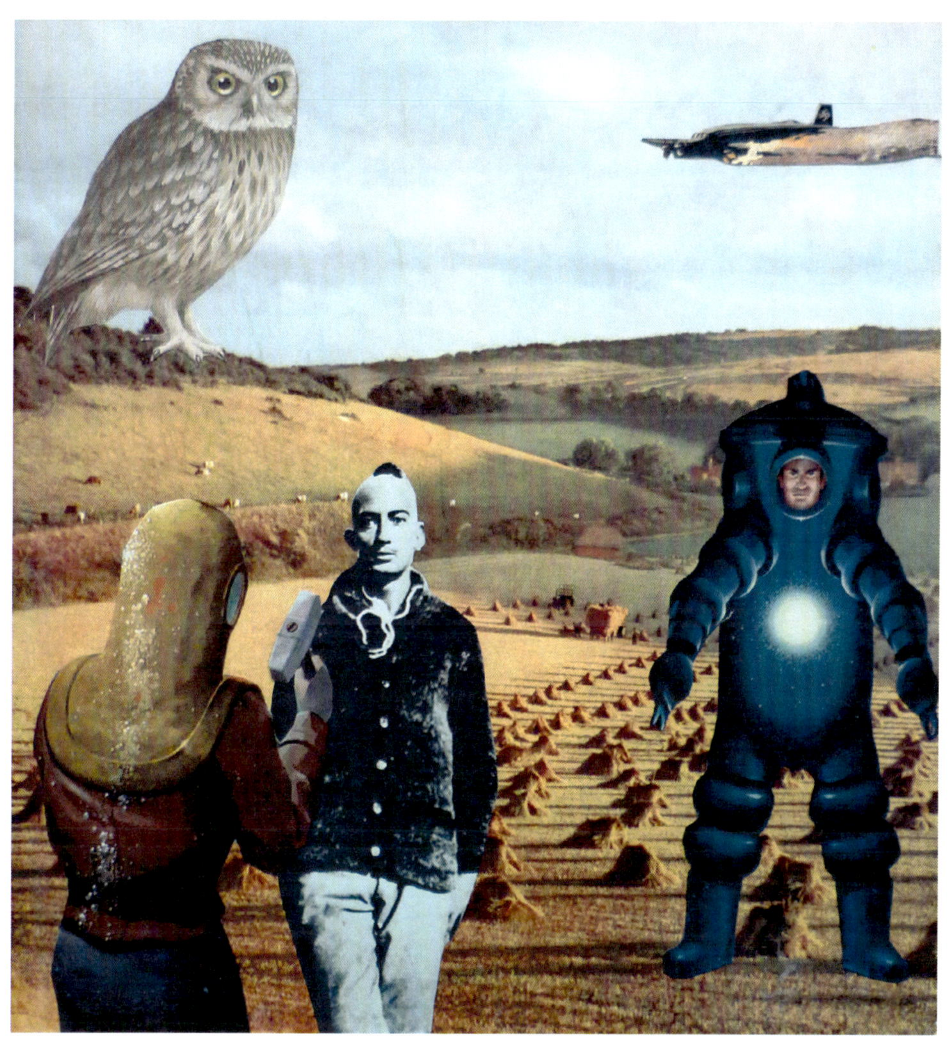

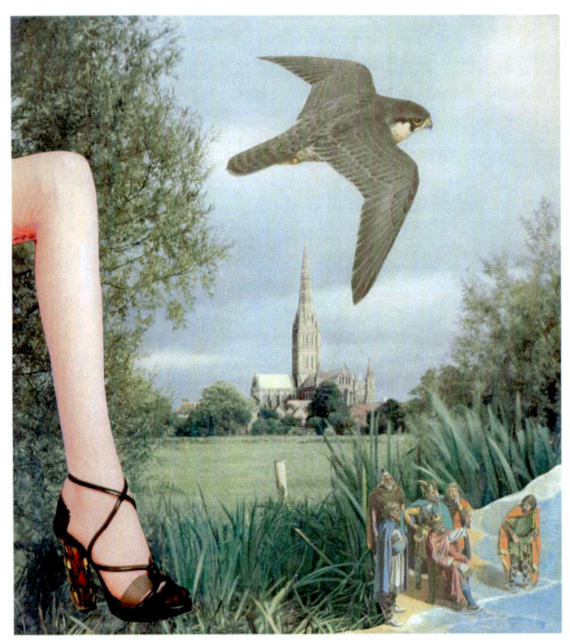

Above:
The Final Proof of Inferiority (2010)
collage 27 x 26 cm

Opposite:
The Edible Critic (2010)
collage 27 x 26 cm

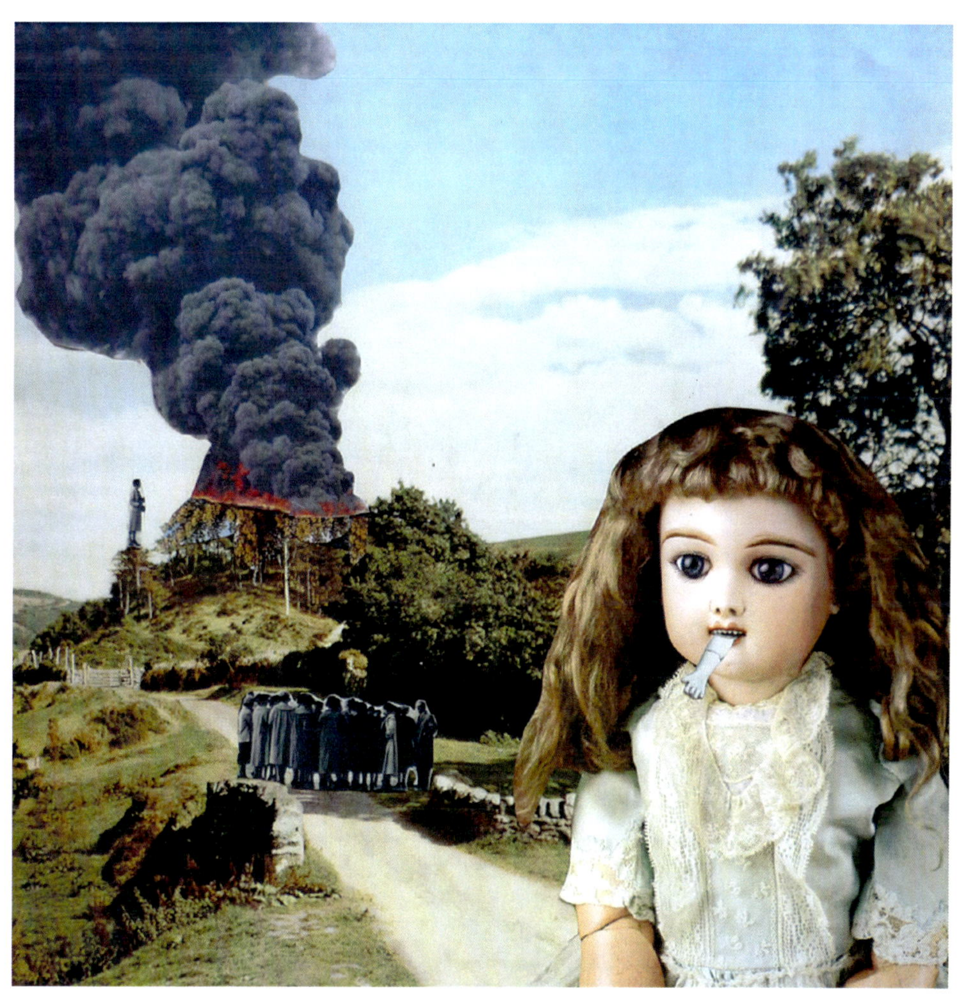

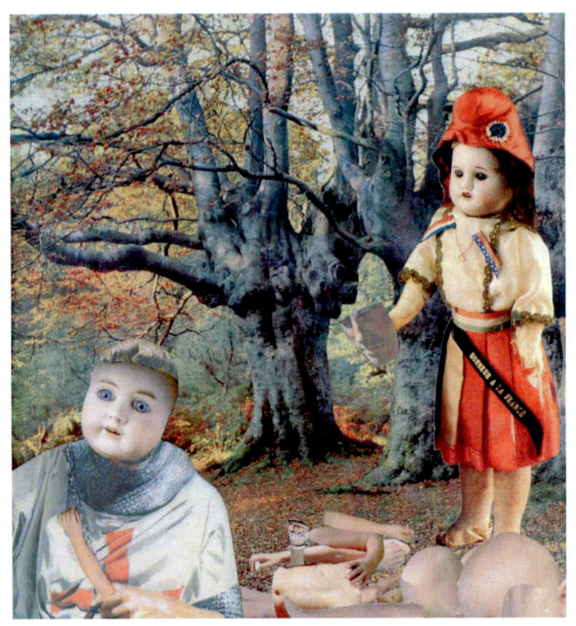

Above:
The Great British Revolution (2010)
collage 27 x 26 cm

Opposite:
The Fire on the Farm (2010)
collage 27 x 26 cm

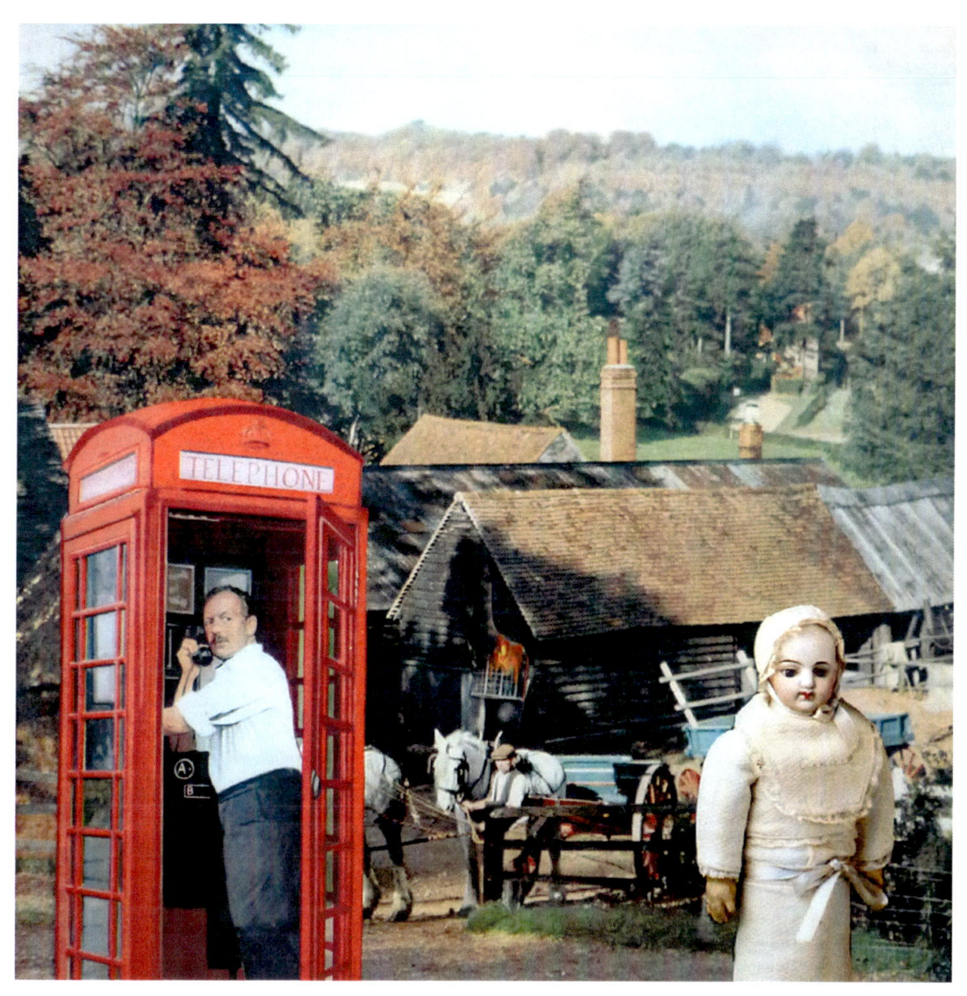

TELEPHONE
A
B

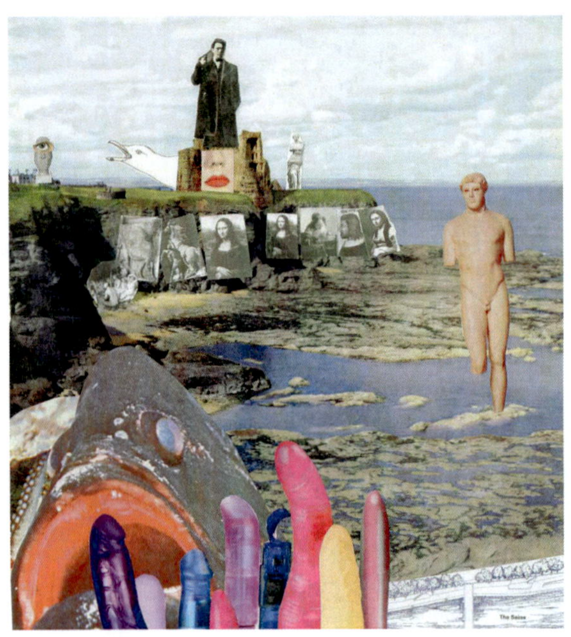

Above:
The Import of Ideology (2010)
collage 27 x 26 cm

Opposite:
The Fortress Island (2010)
collage 27 x 26 cm

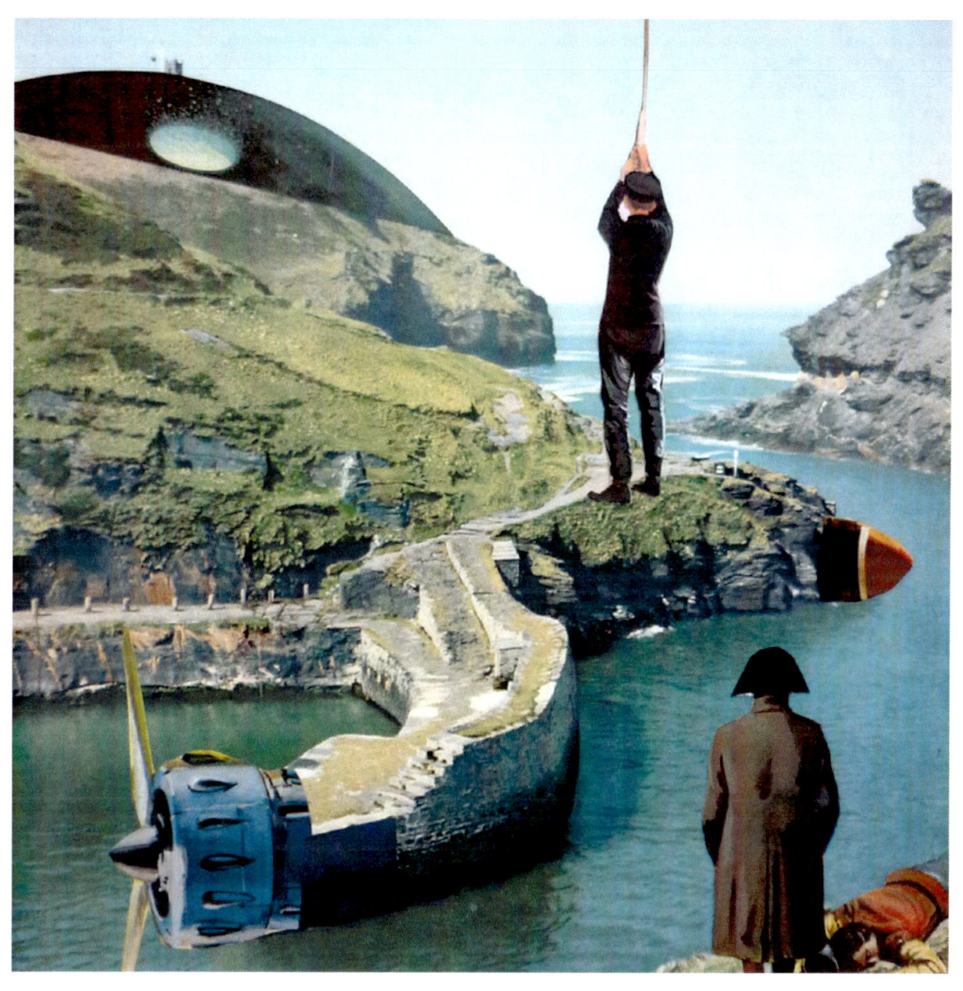

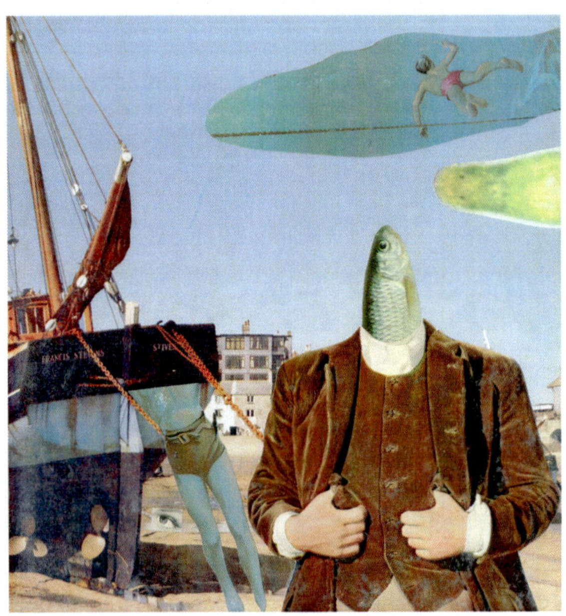

Above:
The Right to Rule by Natural Selection (2010)
collage 27 x 26 cm

Opposite:
The Death of Thatcherism in Britannia (2010)
collage 27 x 26 cm

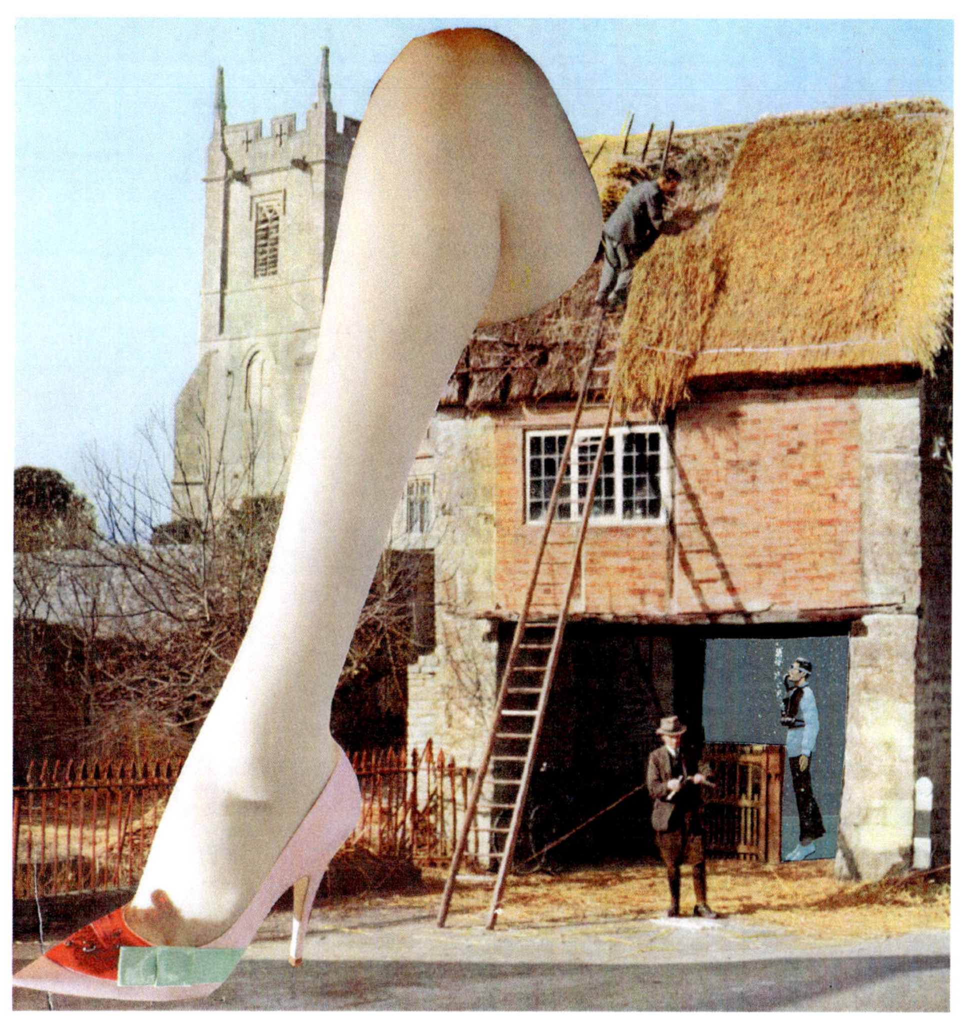

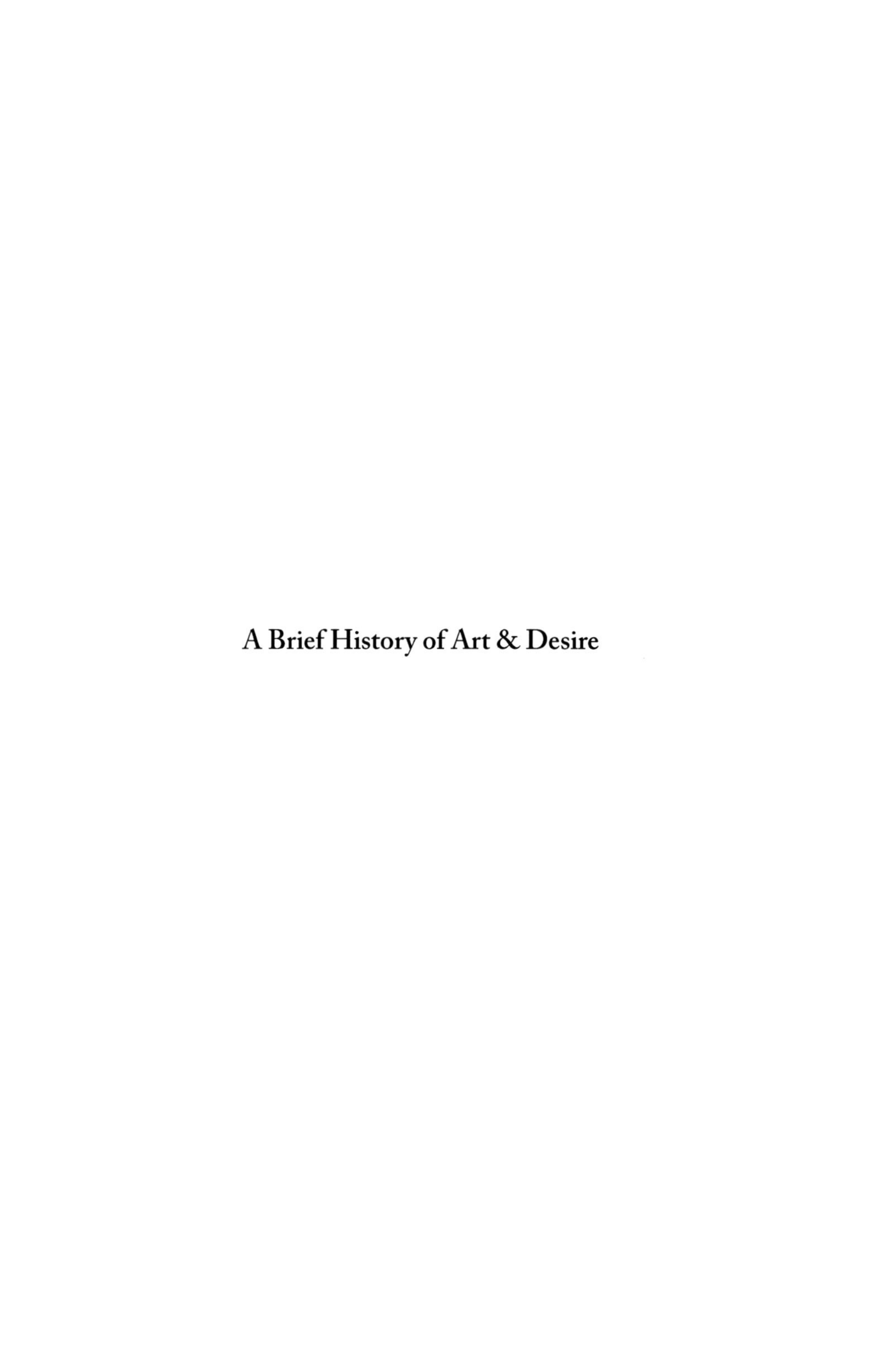

A Brief History of Art & Desire

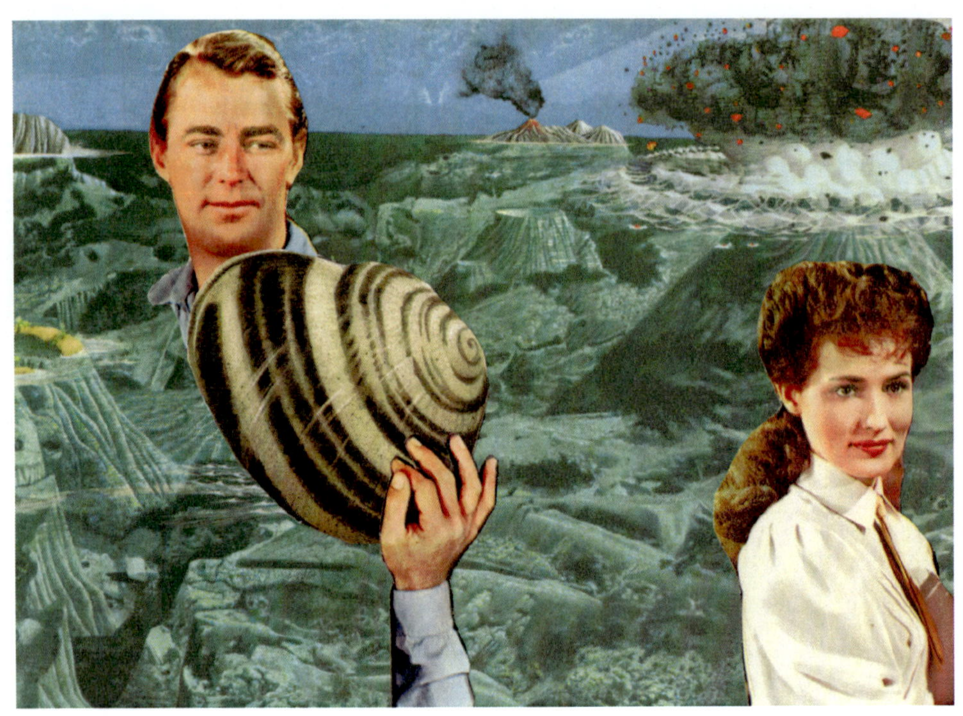

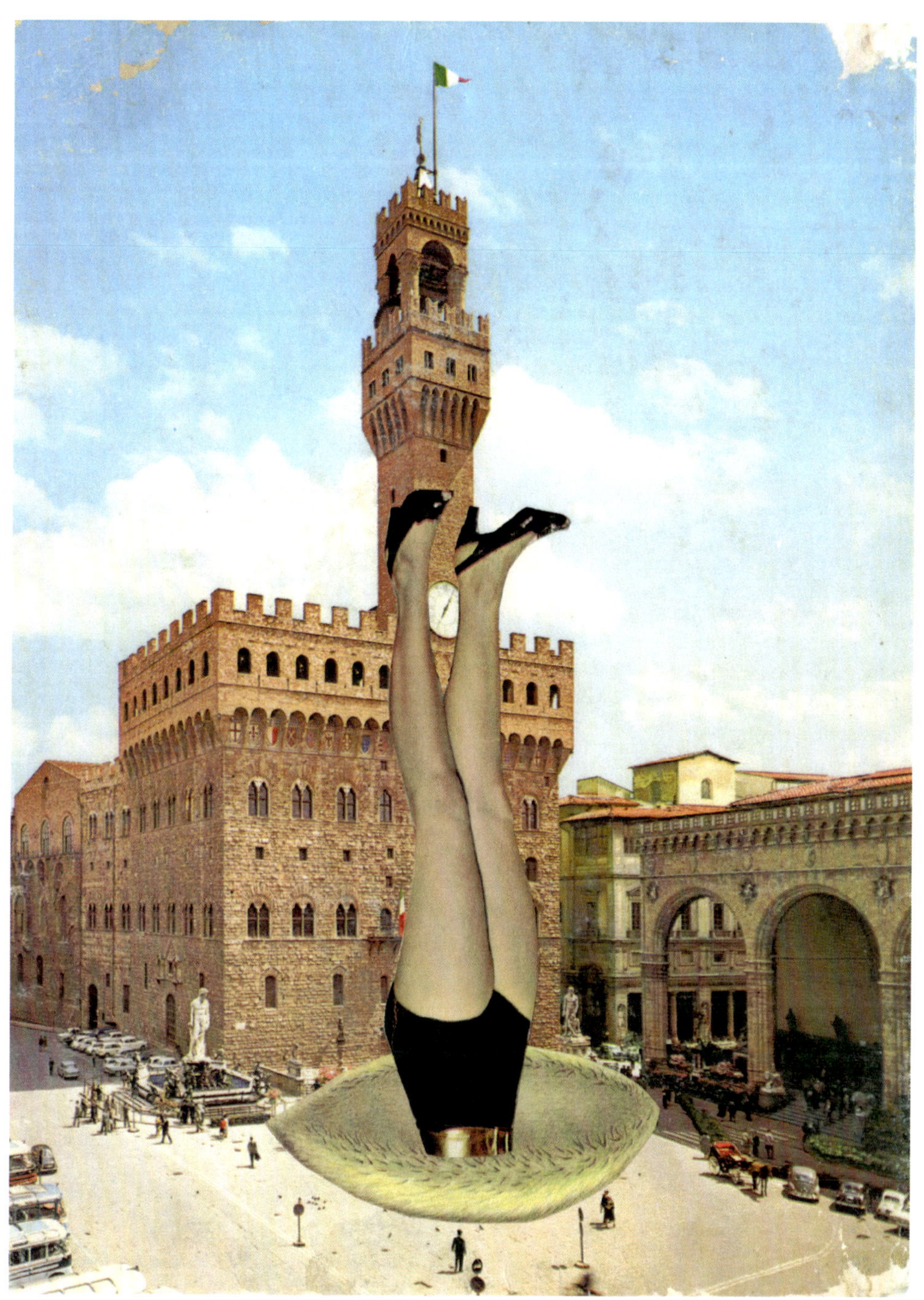

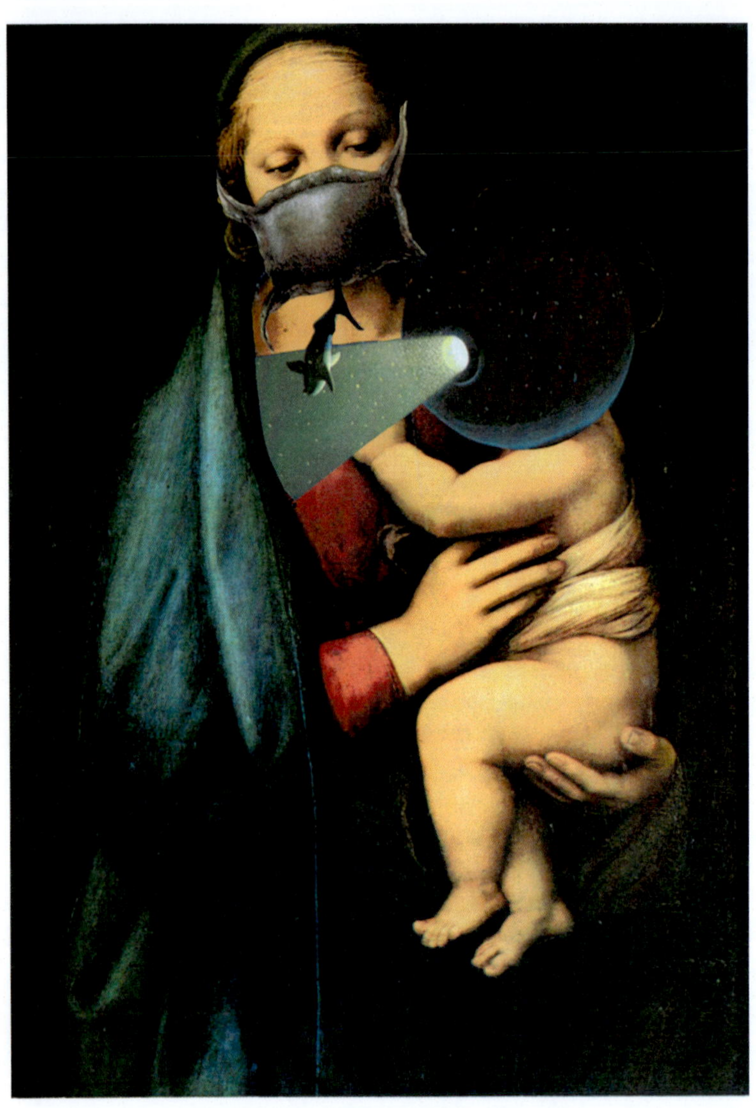

Above:
The Mysteries of the Mermaid's Purse (2012)
collage 24 x 17 cm

Opposite:
Kali Dollies (2012)
collage and ink 26 x 20 cm

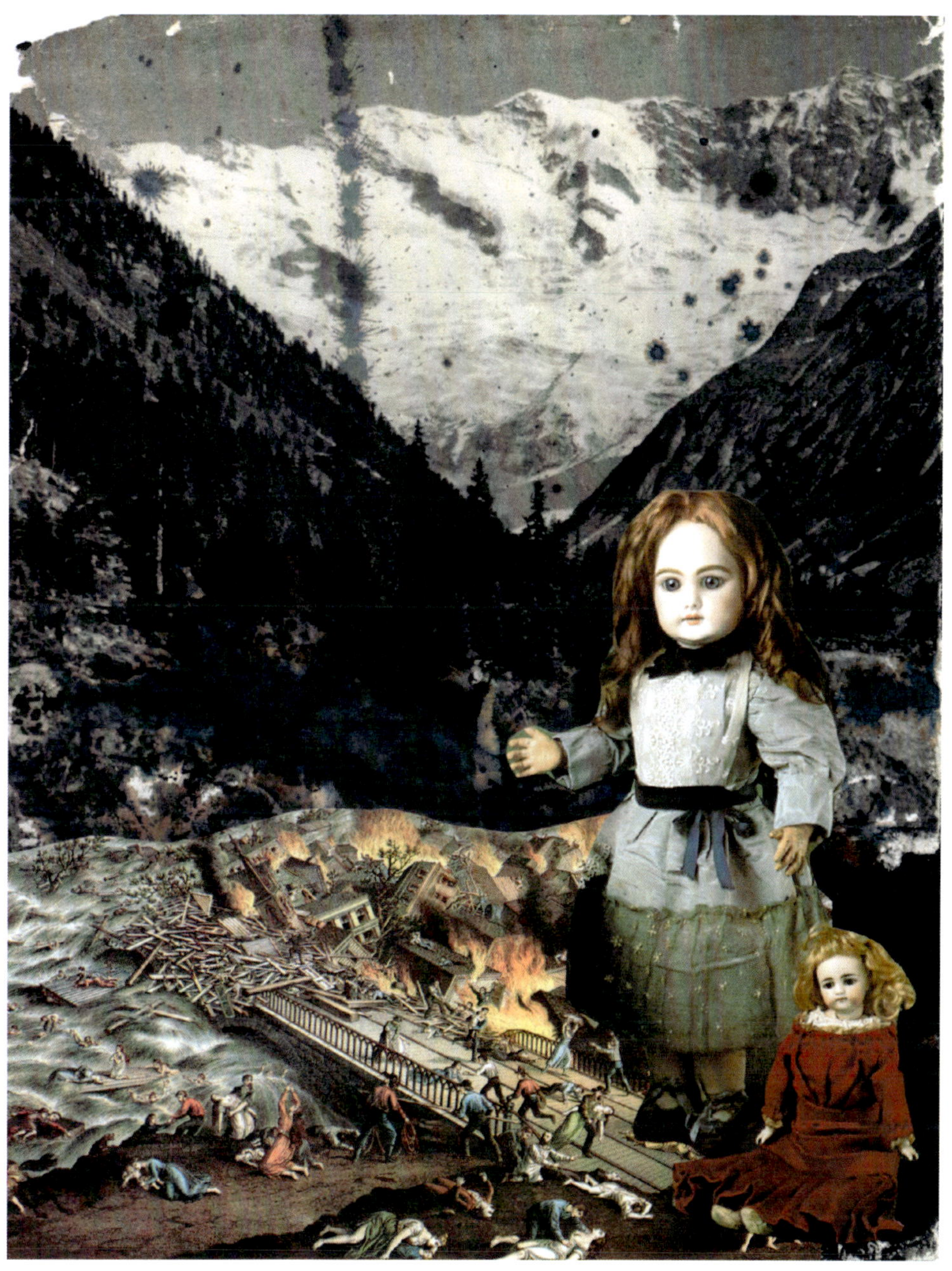

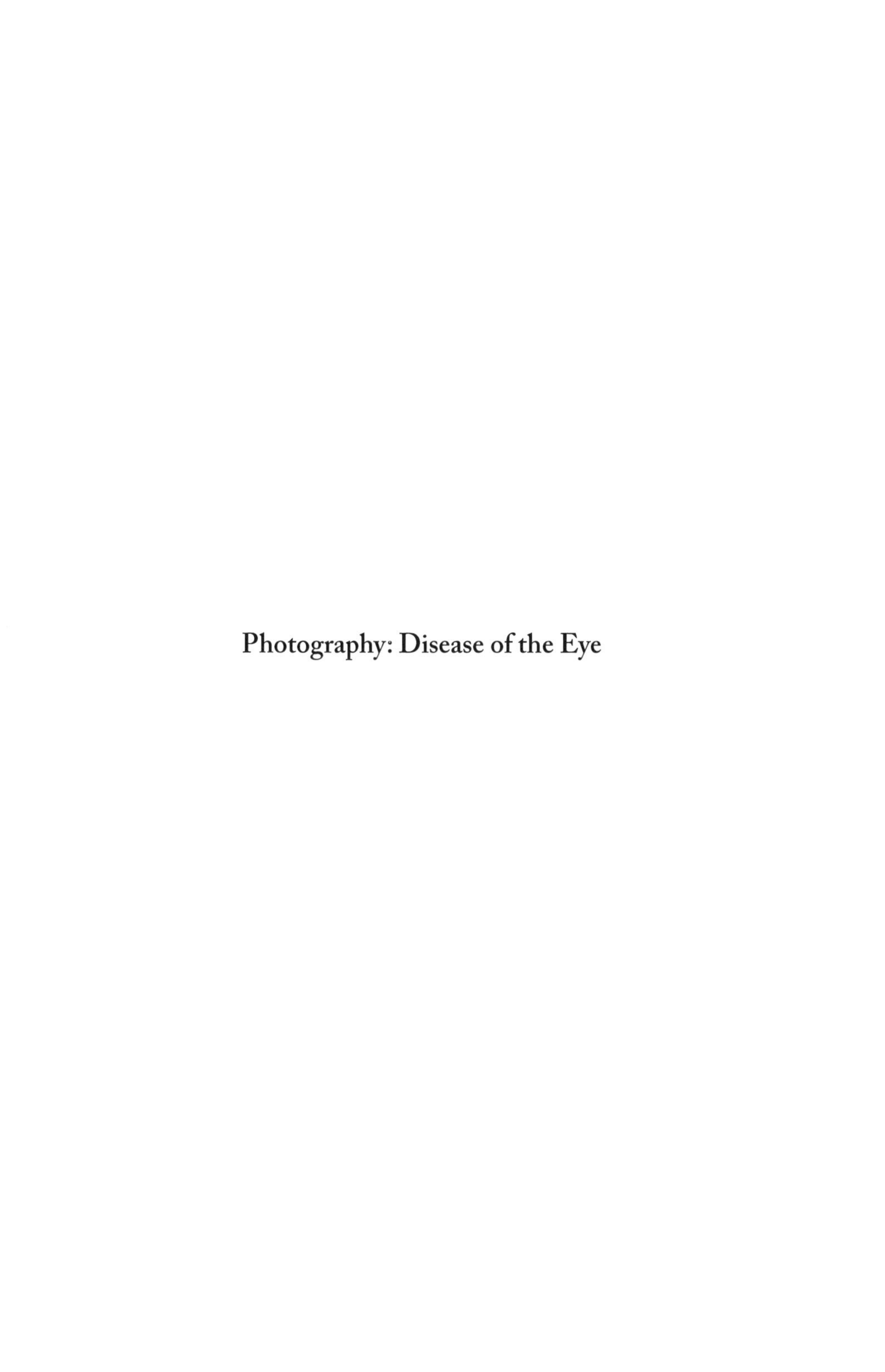

Photography: Disease of the Eye

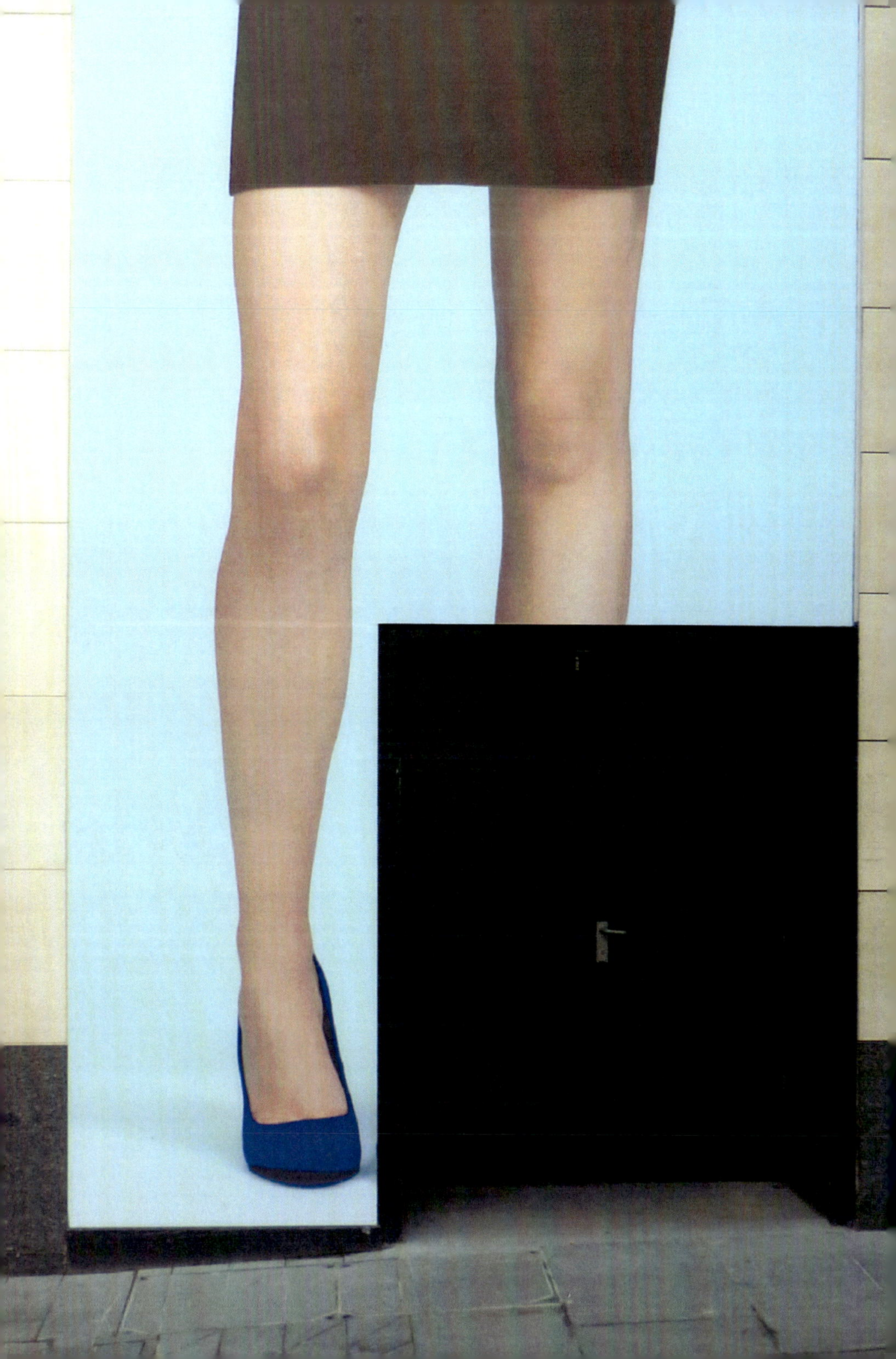

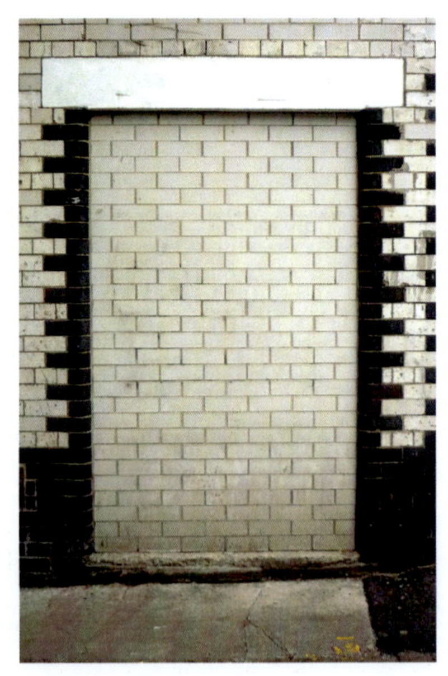

Above:
Senile Cataract (Liverpool, 2011)
C-Type Print 31 x 25 cm

Opposite:
Congenital Cataract (Birmingham, 2011)
C-Type Print 31 x 25 cm

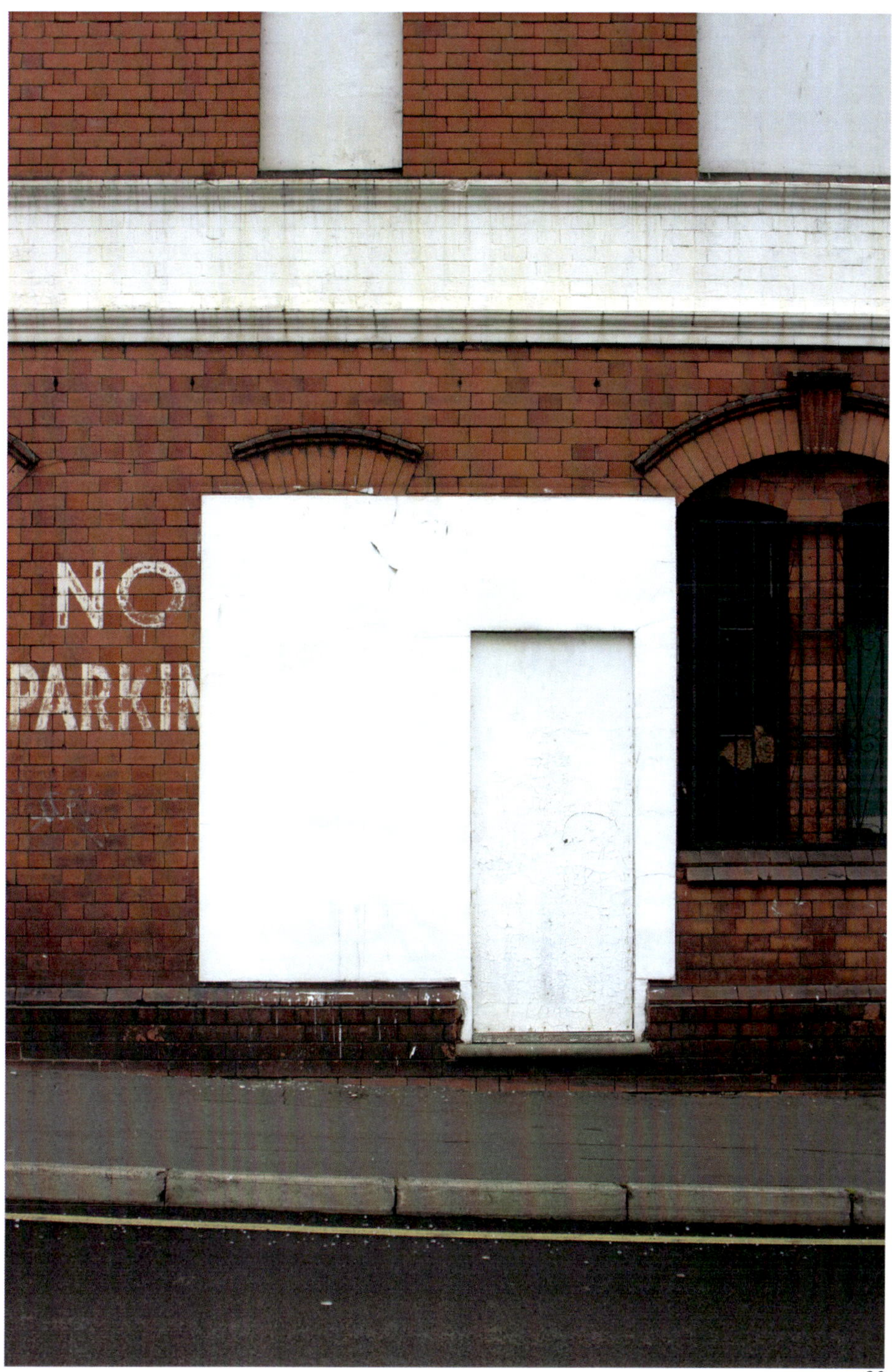

NO
PARKIN

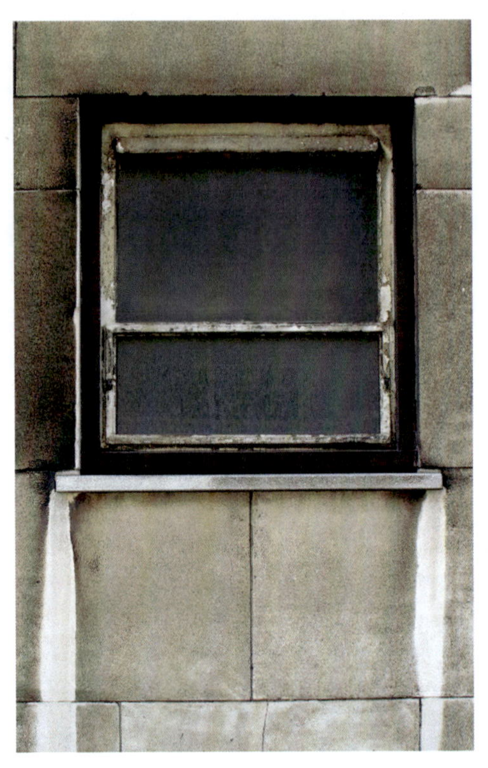

Above:
Dacryphilia (Leeds, 2012)
C-Type Print 31 x 25 cm

Opposite:
Anisocoria (Paris, 2010)
C-Type Print 31 x 25 cm

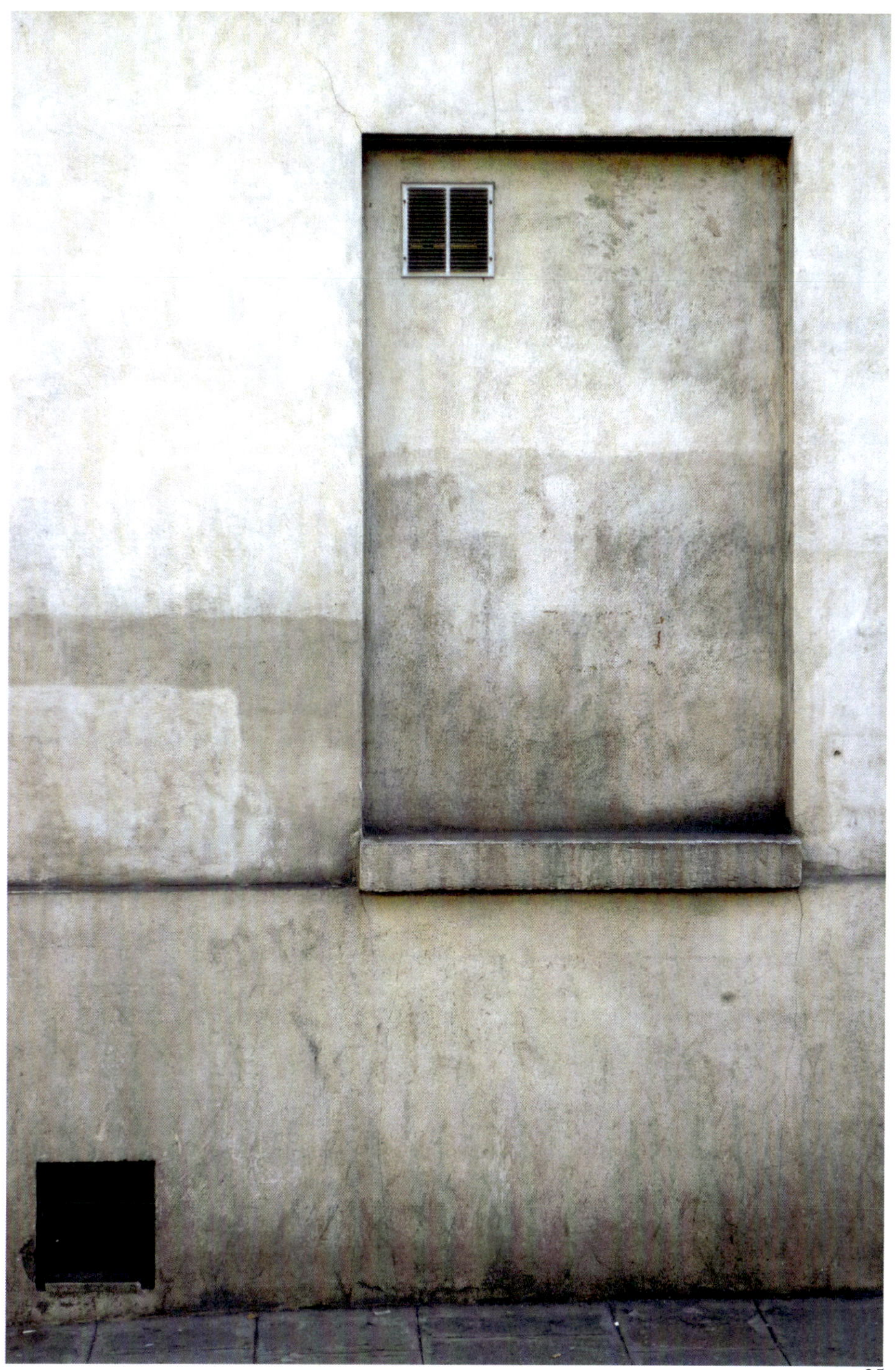

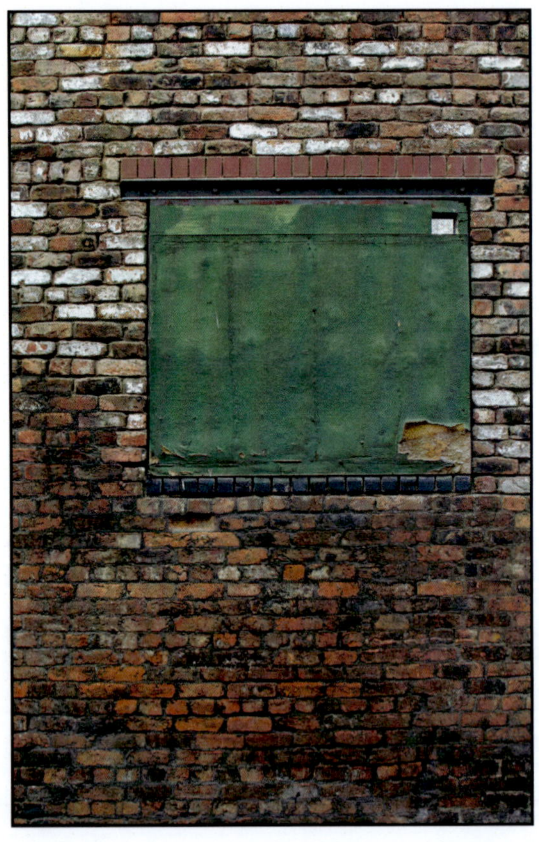

Above:
Ptosis (Liverpool, 2012)
C-Type Print 31 x 25 cm

Opposite:
Optical Occlusion (Liverpool, 2010)
C-Type Print 31 x 25 cm

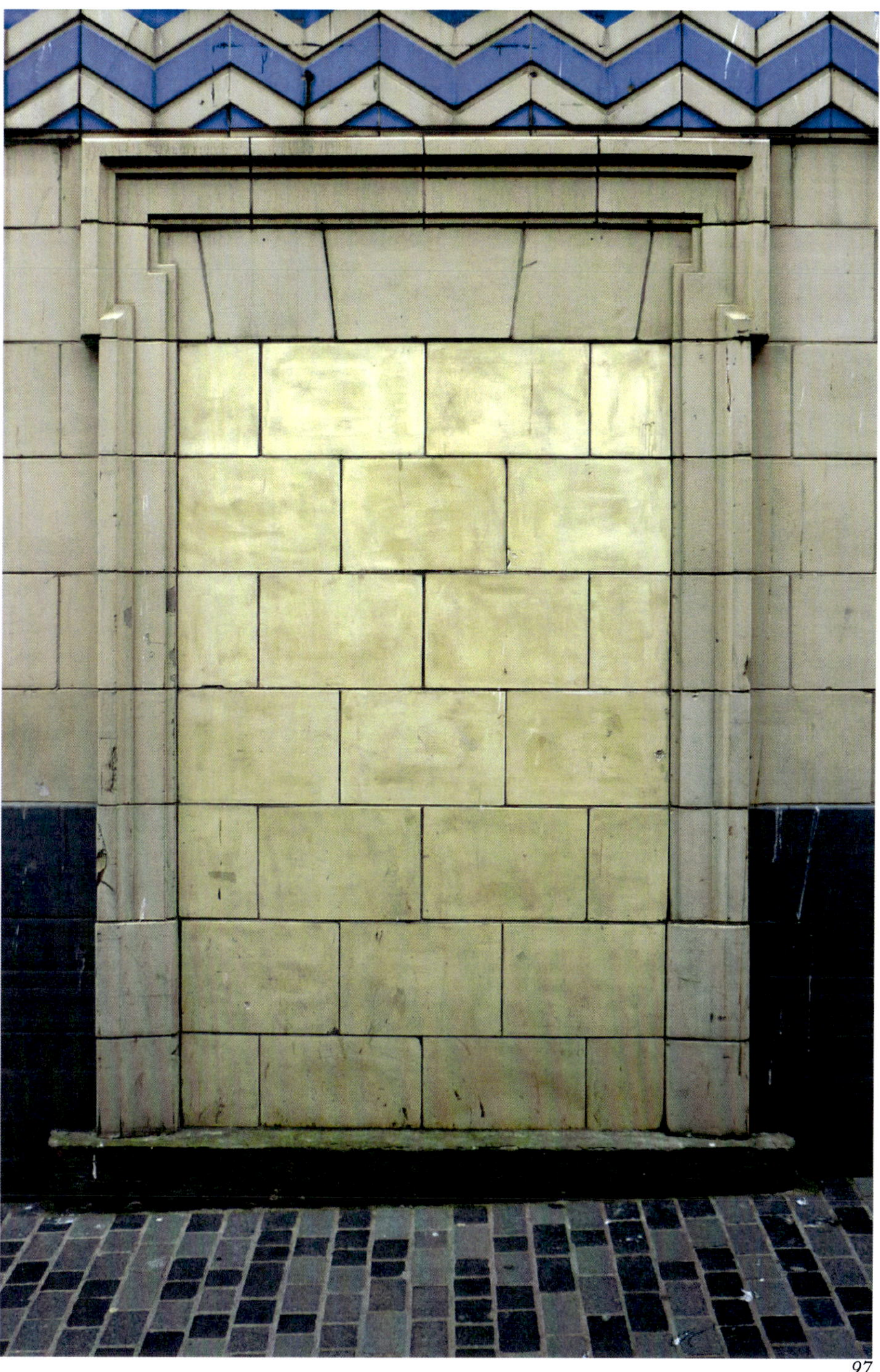

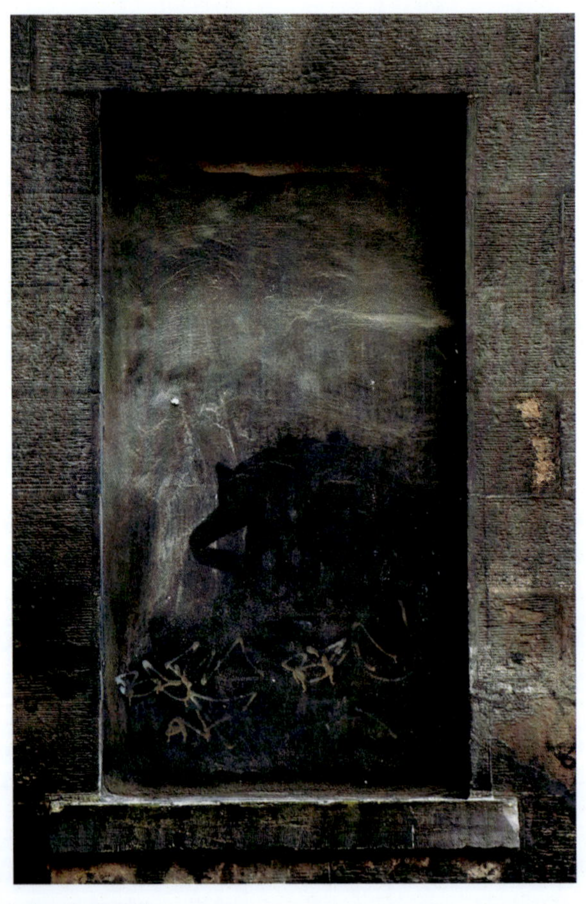

Above:
Congenital Blindness (Edinburgh, 2010)
C-Type Print 31 x 25 cm

Opposite:
Obsessive Compulsive Disorder (Saltaire, 2012)
C-Type Print 31 x 25 cm

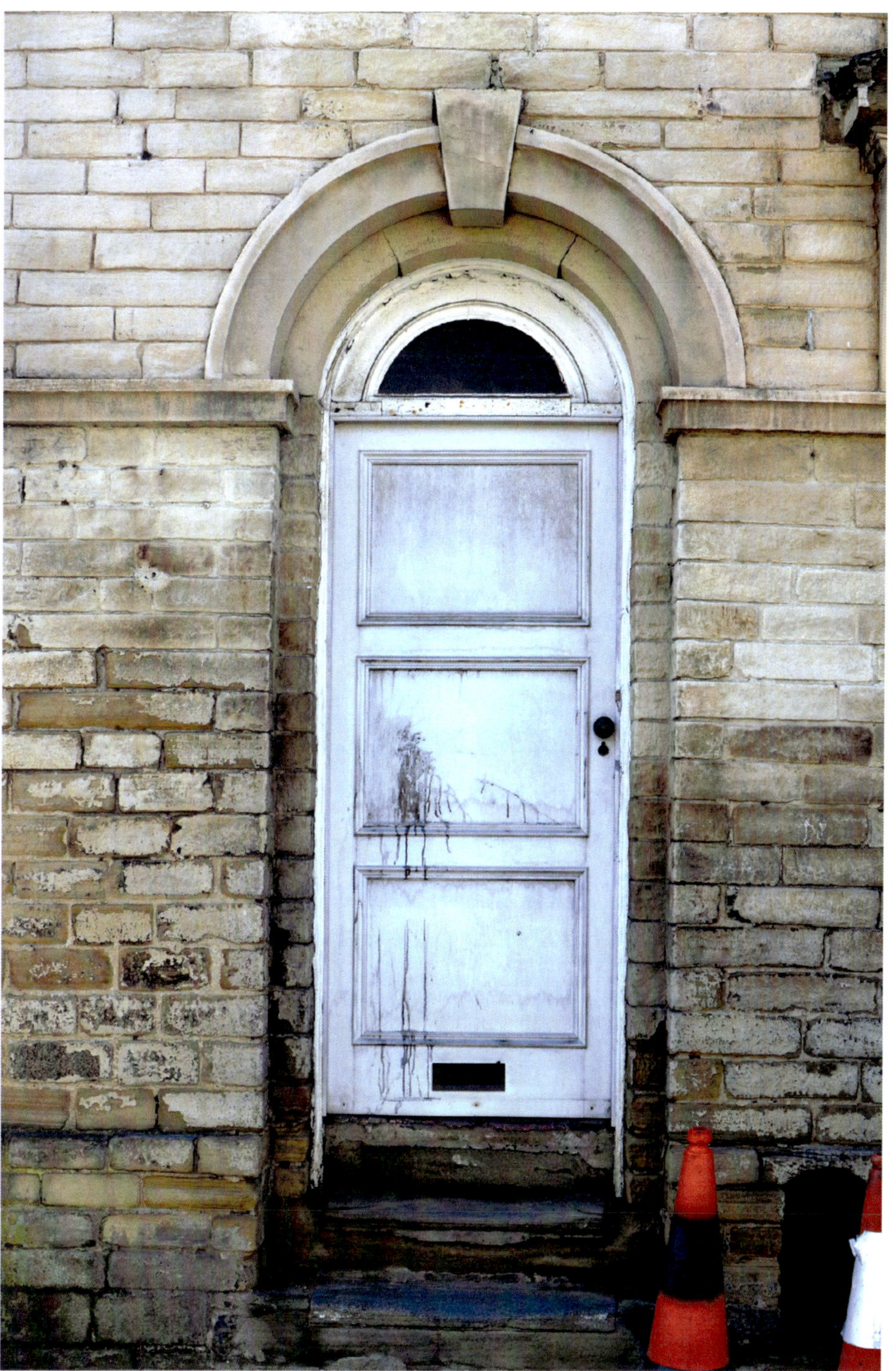

Above:
Dysmetria (Liverpool, 2011)
C-Type Print 25 x 25 cm

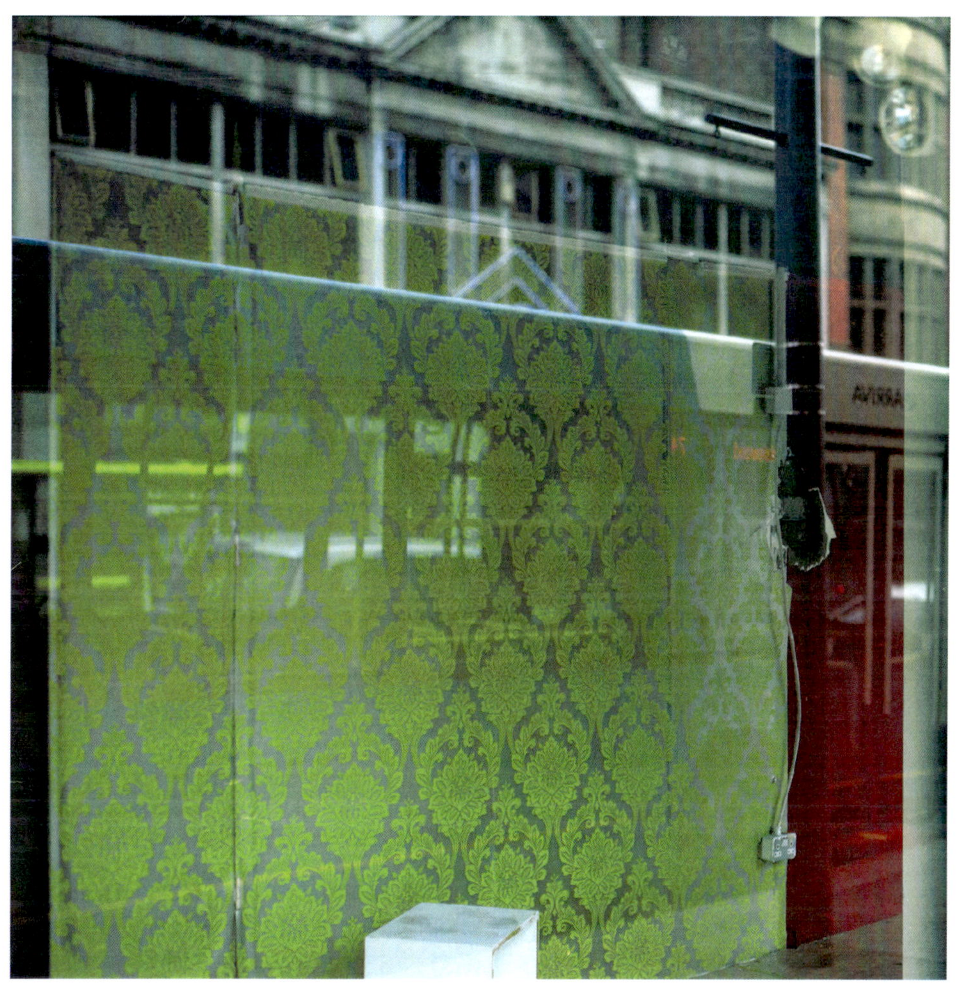

Above:
Dyscalculia (Liverpool, 2011)
C-Type Print 25 x 25 cm

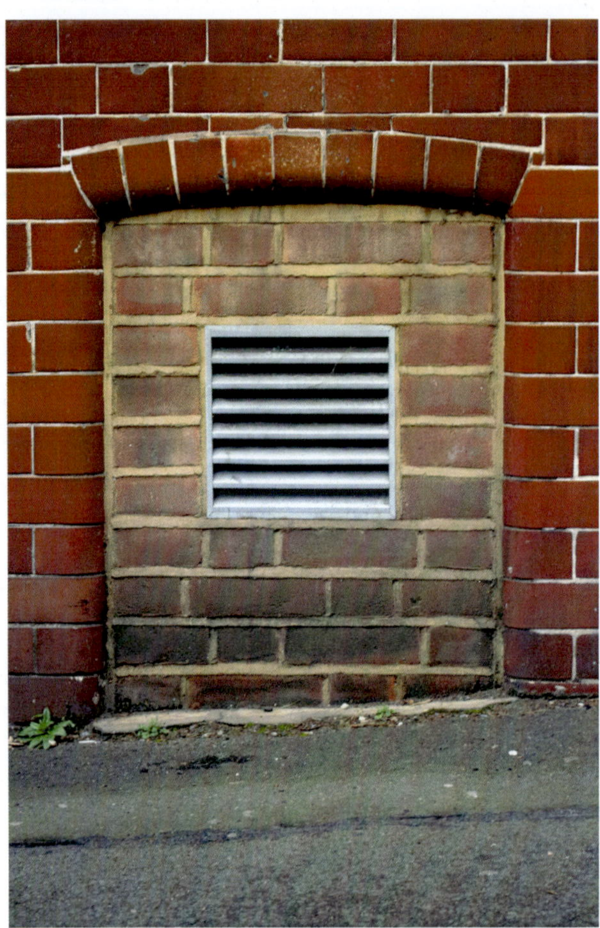

Above:
Conjunctivitis (London, 2011)
C-Type Print 31 x 25 cm

Opposite:
Nyctalopia (Edinburgh, 2010)
C-Type Print 31 x 25 cm

This work was first shown at Bodelwyddan Castle

With thanks to

Krzysztof Fijalkowski
Catriona McAra
Iolo Williams at the Arts Council of Wales
Morrigan Mason at Bodelwyddan Castle
Surrealists of the world

Ruth, George, Daisy & Ted

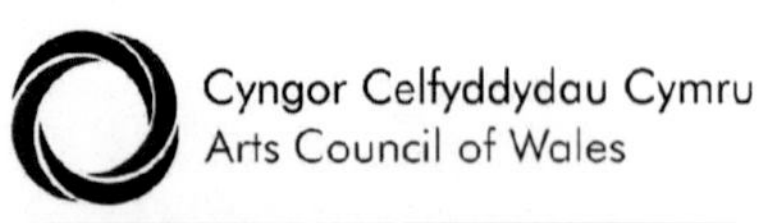

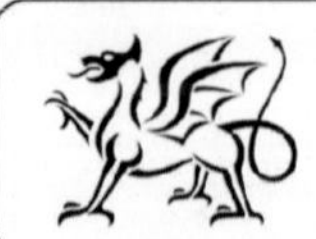

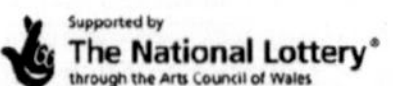